# Mastering College Musical Theatre Auditions

## *Sound Advice for the Student, Teacher, and Parent*

By: David Sisco & Laura Josepher

Authors: David Sisco & Laura Josepher
Cover Design: Matthias Kern
Photo Credits: Dan Mayers (cover), Maria Postigo (back)

Edition: 1:1

10-digit ISBN: 0692910026
13-digit ISBN: 978-0692910023

For information about this book, contact:
Contemporary Musical Theatre Corp.
info@contemporarymusicaltheatre.com

Printed in the United States of America

*Dedicated to Tom Gualtieri,
our dear collaborator and friend.
Thank you for your years of generosity and love.*


*And to Juan Brea,
for your brilliant mind and kind heart.*

# Mastering College
# Musical Theatre Auditions

## *Sound Advice for the Student, Teacher, and Parent*

PREFACE
ACKNOWLEDGEMENTS

## PREFACE

She had a lovely voice. We think. It was hard to tell. She was so nervous after talking to the pianist that she forgot to introduce herself, which only made her more nervous. We tried to put her at ease, but by that point, it was hard talking her off the ledge. Was she unprepared? Did she lack talent? Did she feel pressure to do well for herself? For her parents? For her teachers? It was impossible to tell. Unfortunately, she was unable to show us who she was as a musical theatre performer.

This is not uncommon. There are so many moving parts to an audition and most anything can go wrong. And if you're auditioning for upwards of twenty institutions (as many high school students do), the odds are that something will go wrong at some point: you're sick during the audition, your audition pianist isn't the strongest player, you didn't prepare the proper audition material, etc... It's a challenge to navigate the rocky landscape of college musical theatre auditions.

Add to this the unfortunate fact that musical theatre programs have become increasingly competitive. Some programs only take 12-14 students per class, making the odds slim. Other programs, while bigger, are just as competitive in different ways, depending on the kind of degree they offer and what they're looking for in auditioning students.

But, if you are reading this book, we're guessing it's because you (or someone you know) are serious about training as a musical theatre performer. You won't let these obstacles stand in the way. While it might be daunting, it's completely possible to have a good experience auditioning for college programs. It simply requires time, organization, and good communication skills (with a liberal helping of talent, of course).

Much has been written for the professional about how to give a strong musical theatre audition. There are some fantastic resources out there - good reminders of what to do and not do. But there isn't a comprehensive "go to" resource for the high school student auditioning for college musical theatre programs, let alone supporting advice for their teacher(s) and parents.

As we started writing this book, we understood why. Everyone has to know a substantial amount of information for the auditioning student to be successful. As a colleague once said to us, "Want to know what you don't know? Write a book!" She was dead right. We knew a lot, but we were surprised by the things we didn't know, sitting behind the audition table.

Who's "we"? David Sisco and Laura Josepher. We run ContemporaryMusicalTheatre.com in conjunction with other facets of our busy careers as theatre artists.

David has taught at Marymount Manhattan College, Wagner College's Summer Musical Theatre Institute, and leads master classes and workshops around the country and internationally. For several years, he both played and adjudicated auditions for Marymount, other college programs, and for professional casting. He also musical directs and is a commissioned composer in the genres of classical music and musical theatre. He made his Carnegie Hall and Lincoln Center debuts within 6 months of each other, and won the 2010 NATS Composition Award for his song cycle *Missed Connections*, settings of craigslist posts for mezzo-soprano. David received a BA in Vocal Performance and Composition Honors from Syracuse University and a MM in Vocal Performance from Boston University.

Laura is an active director, teacher, and audition coach, who has worked with students auditioning for performing arts middle schools, high schools, and colleges. She also maintains a thriving freelance directing career, having worked in New York as well as many of the country's leading regional theatres. Laura has a background in developing new plays and musicals, and has taught college students how to collaborate with living writers. She received a BM in Musical Theatre performance and a MA in Educational Theatre, both from New York University.

We have an organic passion for teaching, and love sharing that knowledge. We wrote this book for you, hoping it will give you a leg up on the competition and make everyone feel more at ease about the long journey ahead.

Each chapter highlights a common question we believe the student should ask themselves when preparing for this journey. After an introduction, the chapters are divided into three separate sections: one for the student, one for the teacher, and one for the parents. You're welcome to read everything, but we offer specific advice to each audience in the individual sections.

This book has been vetted by theatre administrators, voice teachers, acting teachers, high school students, and parents who are very familiar with the challenges of auditioning for musical theatre programs. We believe our background and their combined insights will make this a very useful book to you.

So, whether you're a high school student with dreams of going to college for musical theatre, or you're a teacher or parent looking to support a young artist, this book will help you navigate everything from choosing where to apply, to what (not) to sing at the audition.

We're happy to be part of that process!

David Sisco & Laura Josepher
New York City

## ACKNOWLEDGEMENTS

It seemed audacious to write a book. Who does that? But the more we got to thinking about it, the more we realized we had a lot of valuable thoughts we wanted to share. We have amazing colleagues, friends, and families in our lives, who listened and helped us shape this book into something beyond what we had initially imagined. We're glad to have an opportunity to publicly acknowledge these beautiful individuals.

The first person to see our thoughtful (yet completely disorganized) musings ended up being our editor. Neil Gordon, you are such a kind and talented man. Thank you for giving us perspective on what we had and how to better mold it into something more meaningful.

As we said in the Preface, we asked many people from several different backgrounds to read this book to give you the best possible picture of how to prepare for auditions. The following people generously donated their time and helpful input: AJ Cali, Lisa Cali, Kevin Connell, Tom Gualtieri, Ally Gray, Lynn Gray, Nina Kauffman, Andy Mank, Gaby Mank, Sylvan Oswald, Dr. Jennifer Sgroe, and Heidi Siegell.

A special thanks to Andy Mank for his invaluable insights on the audition process from a parent's perspective; to Rusty Curcio for sharing his vast knowledge about preparing for dance auditions; and to Kevin Connell for his overarching knowledge and input.

We thank the following musical theatre students, who shared with us things they'd wished they'd known going into auditions: Courtney Allen, Amanda Garcia-Walker, Thomas Kuklenski, Gaby Mank, Nicolette Minella, Brandon Santoro, Sarah Van Zwoll, Alicia Vitale and Samantha Weathersby.

Thanks to our great photographers, Dan Mayers (cover) Maria Postigo (authors' photo), and to Alexandra Foucard, Tom Gualtieri, and Marisa Miranda for being part of our cover photo shoot. We're grateful for Matthias Kern's awesome cover design. Our special thanks to Roberto Araujo for your keen eye.

The Drama Book Shop in New York City was an amazing resource for us as we researched and wrote this book. Thanks to the knowledgeable and friendly staff.

Thanks to Betty Ciacchi for her sound legal advice and consistent support. Thanks to Scott Charlton at M&T Bank and Kurt Jordan at SCORE for believing in our company and for their guiding hands.

We stand on the strong shoulders of our teachers. David wishes to recognize all his public school music educators for their knowledge and tireless dedication: Nancy Congdon, Mary Schroyer, David Schroyer, Martha Skovenski, and Thomas Voorhies. He is also grateful to Dr. Joseph Downing, Dr. Carl Johengen, Shiela Kibbe, and Dr. Julianna Sabol, who molded him as a teaching artist. Laura wishes to thank her mentors Stephen Palestrant, Lowell & Nancy Swortzell, and Fred Silver. And also to Sue Lawless, who continues to be a role model for how to work and teach with kindness.

We also thank our amazing families, who have sacrificed for our happiness and given us the courage to leap into the unknown. David thanks his mom and dad, Carole and Warren Sisco, his sister Jennifer Burgy, brother-in-law Paul Burgy, and two awesome nieces, Carly & Kelsey Burgy. Laura thanks her brilliant husband, Juan Brea, who always knew when it was time to step in and help, as well as when to step back and let us fly on our own. Laura also wants to thank her two amazing daughters, Chelsea and Sadie, who continue to teach her every day, And lastly Laura would like to thank her parents, Barbara and Tony Josepher for sharing their love of the arts.

We are surrounded with stunning colleagues and friends. While we can't name them all, we wish to recognize some of them here. David is grateful for Lael Atkinson, Sam Clover, Susan Fenley, Alexandra Foucard, Danita Geltner, Thomas Gentile, Lesley

Mazzotta, Patricia Miller, Elizabeth Mondragon, Marshall Sampson, Lisa Smith, and Korland Simmons. Laura would like to thank Bob Dillon and Matthias Kern (the two best friends a girl could have), Halla Elias, and her "mom squads," both in NYC and The Catskills.

And to our beautiful colleague and friend, Tom Gualtieri. May you all be blessed to have a collaborator with such tremendous knowledge, wit, and grace.

# Mastering College Musical Theatre Auditions

*Sound Advice for the Student, Teacher, and Parent*

By: David Sisco & Laura Josepher

# CHAPTER 1: DO I REALLY WANT TO MAJOR IN MUSICAL THEATRE?

This is the single most important question you can ask yourself. There are so many things you need to become aware of when pursuing a degree in musical theatre. College auditions are a very expensive proposition. It takes a lot of time and hard work just to get into a college musical theatre program. Once you're in, the training is incredibly intense. Then there's the question of if, how, where, and when you will work in the industry once you've graduated.

We realize this isn't the most upbeat way to start a book. We're not two jaded New Yorkers trying to squash your dreams by telling you, "This is hard, kid!" If you're reading this, you clearly have a passion for musical theatre, and that's awesome. We do, however, want to help open your eyes to the full picture of what it takes to be a musical theatre performer in this ever-changing industry.

We're going to break down each of the challenges for you so you understand the full weight of this decision.

## Expense

Being a musical theatre artist is a costly venture at any stage of your development. You need voice lessons, acting classes, dance classes, and sometimes an audition coach. There are other expenses, such as headshots, purchasing music, plays, and proper dance attire (good tap shoes are expensive!). And what if you want to attend a summer program to better prepare yourself for the realities of a career as a performer (and you should)? They cost thousands of dollars! And many high school students do more than one intensive prior to auditioning for college.

And that's just the tip of the iceberg. Then there's the expense of applying to and auditioning at each college. When you apply, you will have to pay an application fee. These range from $30 - $75. Many students apply to upwards of 20 schools because musical theatre degree programs are so competitive. That's literally hundreds of dollars spent before you even sing a note!

What about travel, hotels, and meals? Ideally, you'll go to the school for your audition (or travel to a regional audition or unified). And you may want to visit the college before you decide to apply to get a better sense of whether or not it's right for you. That's more money.

While you're in school, you'll continue to spend extra money on voice lessons, dance classes (many programs have additional fees built in for this training), sheet music, audition outfits, and much more. Sometimes your financial aid will cover these expenses. Sometimes you'll have to foot the bill.

And we're sorry to tell you the expenses don't end when you graduate from college. You'll constantly be investing in new classes, lessons, coachings, updated headshots, music, plays…. It's literally endless.

Are you collectively ready for these expenses? This is an unfortunate reality of a life in the arts and everyone has to be on board if you are to be successful.

*Time Commitment*

Being a musical theater performer takes unwavering commitment over countless hours. Many start training before they're in middle school. Beyond the sheer amount of hours it takes to attend classes in the three disciplines that make up the art form of musical theatre (voice, acting, dance), there needs to be an almost equal number of hours set aside for research and practice.

And what is practice? It's not just running through your song, monologue, or reviewing the steps to a dance. It is the systematic taking apart of the material so you can fully incorporate it into your body. And when you practice, you're not just working on the material. You're also focusing on the fundamental techniques that allow you to bring life to a piece: breath, diction, movement, etc…

4

Many people can perform, but not everyone can perform well. What separates the two is practice, which is often tedious.

We'll talk about how to prepare audition material later in the book, but you should expect it to take about a month to properly learn and embody one song or monologue. That means 4 weeks of 1 hour practice sessions at least 5 times a week - about 20 hours of private work in addition to lessons or class. And you'll need to learn a lot of material to meet the different audition requirements of the institutions where you're applying.

If you don't have the constitution or time management skills to pursue this course of study, this is not the major for you. It only gets harder from here on out.

*Training*

One of our biggest challenges is explaining to high school students the difference between the joy of working on the school musical versus the demanding training that comes with being a singing actor. We all have wonderful memories of the shows we've worked on: the inside jokes, the applause... it's great. But when going to college for musical theatre performance, you will receive intensive training in voice, drama, and dance. It's less romantic a process. In fact, it's an incredibly challenging major that will use every part of your body and brain. It's very much like training for the Olympics: the schedule is exhausting; you'll be pushed to (and often beyond) your limits; the competition is fierce; and constructive feedback can at times be blunt and feel very personal.

This training will not only push you physically, it will force you to confront mental and emotional walls most people try to avoid. These walls must be torn down if people are going to believe you as a character in a musical. There's no hiding when it comes to emotional honesty, which can only come from exploring the thorny underbelly of your own personal desires and fears.

Are you willing to be involved in a training program that demands these things of you?

5

As our colleague Jason Forbach (who recently played Enjolras in the Broadway production of *Les Misérables*) told us in an interview, "There's a difference between wanting to be the star and being a working actor."

For many actors, Broadway is a dream, not a reality. Instead, they cobble together a career working off-Broadway, regionally, on film, television, and voiceovers. The goal of any training program should be to make you a versatile, working actor. If you get to Broadway, consider yourself lucky. But that shouldn't be your goal. Your goal should simply be to make a living doing what you love. And that's no easy task.

Do you know how many actors are out of work at this very moment? According to Actors' Equity Association (the actors' union), only 42% of their membership worked in the 2015-2016 season (that's 17,834 members out of about 51,000). Of that percentage, 15% of those were not actors, but stage managers. So, that means only 27% of union actors worked that season, and they only worked an average of 17 out of 52 weeks. How's that for sobering?

No one is safe from this reality. Several years ago, Broadway veteran Chuck Cooper (*Caroline, or Change*, *The Life*) did a Q&A with Syracuse University theatre students. When asked the biggest fallacy about being an actor, he said, "That winning a Tony means anything." By this he meant that even a Tony Award (which he received for his performance in *The Life*) isn't enough to create job security for an actor. They must always be hustling for the next job, regardless of where they are in their career. If Meryl Streep is worried about her next job, you can bet you will be too.

And even if you're consistently working, that doesn't mean you're living on easy street. Your entire body is your instrument, and it will need constant tune-ups. We've been interviewing Broadway actors about vocal health issues for the last couple years. In an anonymous survey, 85% of those who participated said it was common for them to feel vocally tired after a week of shows. And almost a quarter of those actors said they had suffered temporary or permanent vocal damage due to a Broadway production. Scary right? This is why training is an ongoing reality for any smart performing artist.

***

Now that we've put all these thoughts in your head, how do you know if this is really what you want to do?

You may not know the answer to this question yet, and that's OK. Sometimes the only way to know for certain is to begin training with professionals who are working in the industry. And training isn't just performing in shows, though that can be part of it. Training should include private lessons and classes.

One of the best ways to find out if this is for you is to attend a summer musical theatre intensive. There are several around the country that will keep you busy from sunrise to sunset with all things musical theatre, including: dance, voice, acting, improv, scene study, and rehearsals for a showcase. This most closely mirrors the intensity of an undergraduate performance program. If you get through two or more weeks of this level of intense training and still think it's what you'd like to do, it may be a positive sign this path is right for you. We'll talk more about summer programs in Chapter 3.

Yes, musical theatre is a very exciting and rewarding career. Yes, you can make a living being a working actor if you get good training and utilize all your skills sets. And yes, this career is as challenging as it seems. If this is what you really want, we want to help you succeed.

## STUDENT

How do you know if you have what it takes to be a successful musical theatre performer? In a lot of cases, you won't know because there are so many variables, many of which are out of your control (you won't have a say in getting cast, right?).

Sit down with your family and teachers to discuss the following questions. They will be good indicators of whether or not this path is right for you:

- Am I willing to work hard?
- Am I (and my family or support system) willing to invest time and money in my study as an artist, knowing it requires a lifetime of training?
- Do I have a clear picture of the challenges facing musical theatre performers (financially and otherwise) in the industry?
- Is there another course of study I'm equally interested in?

If you have an opportunity, speak to a college musical theatre performer to get a more accurate picture of what a "normal" week looks like for them. Talk to a working musical theatre performer about their career, whether or not they rely on a "survival job," and what advice they might have for you. The beautiful thing about this industry is that it's filled with many generous people who are willing to share their thoughts.

If any of this sounds scary and you have other ideas of things you'd like to study, we sincerely suggest you consider pursuing those instead. That doesn't mean you can't continue doing theatre in a different capacity. There are plenty of community and professional theaters that engage people who don't have a BA, BFA, BM, or certificate specializing in musical theatre.

Or maybe you'll consider another major in the arts: directing, stage management, design, or theatre studies. There are so many wonderful ways to specialize in theatre.

Whatever you decide, be open to change. You're in one of the most exciting times in your life, and the trajectory of your personal and professional career may dramatically change in the next four years. Neither of us ended up where we thought we would. David was an aspiring opera singer turned aspiring Broadway performer turned teacher/performer/composer and Laura was an actress, then a stage manager, then a director. The truth is: we couldn't be any happier in our lives. We both have many friends who went to music and theatre school who later became lawyers, doctors, and other non-musical things. All completely happy. Your journey is your journey. Let it help you discover who you are and where you should be. And if that takes you to college for musical theatre, awesome! Read on.

## TEACHER

You are often on the front line with the student, answering questions, giving advice, pointing them in a positive direction. Often our students will tell us things we're sure they don't share with their parents. We take that as a deep bond of trust and work to be worthy of it every day.

Because you're an important part of your student's life, they will probably ask you whether or not they should pursue a career as a musical theatre performer. Or they'll just flat out tell you they're going to do it and ask for your help.

There is something very alluring about musical theatre. Broadway shows are mighty sexy. Just the mention of a show like *Hamilton* might make them gush. But what isn't seen on stage are the millions of collective (often agonizing) hours each creative and performing artist took to get to that particular moment. Not many people think about that (especially students). They just know they're attracted to the world of theatre.

The most important question you can help the student answer is "why?" Why do they want to be a musical theatre performer? If the answer is because they "love it" or "want to be a star on Broadway," it's a safe bet they don't have a clear idea of what the career demands. If possible, connect them with a musical theatre professional so they have a more realistic view of what's required:

9

- A significant financial investment in lessons, classes, and other resources
- Unwavering commitment to training throughout their academic and professional careers
- The fortitude to deal with fierce competition with little job security

As we mentioned, musical theatre is a painfully demanding and competitive field. Even those with successful careers often dabble in other linear vocations: teaching, hair and makeup design, massage therapy, personal training, and web development, among other professions. It's important to help the student outline other places they excel and have a passion while considering a career as a musical theatre performer.

As teachers, we know how hard it is to negotiate the line between being supportive and helping a student come to necessary conclusions about their talent. We believe it's our job as educators to take a student's gifts and hone them. Sometimes there's a natural ability, which makes it abundantly clear the student has a calling for a career in the performing arts. Sometimes the student's love for their craft, however, does not match their talent.

We have to be honest with our students while always letting them know we care.

Sometimes, though, even the best of us don't have enough perspective when it comes to helping a student decide whether or not they can be a successful musical theatre performer. If you're not directly involved with professional musical theatre, you might not know where your student should go to college, what they should sing, or how to choose the best audition cut. That's why we wrote this book. The fact that you're taking the time to read it sets you apart and will hopefully put you in the best position to help your student.

Perhaps there are other resources at your disposal that can supplement your knowledge. Is there a musical theatre professional with considerable experience in your area? We say "considerable experience" because there are a lot of instructors, perhaps well meaning, who don't have the depth of knowledge your student deserves and needs to succeed. Believe us: we've looked at a lot of voice teacher, acting, and vocal coach websites. Everyone is trying to corner the market, claiming to know just what's best for the young performer. Sometimes they can be too wrapped up in their own methodology to see what the young artist actually needs.

Sometimes, we have to be selfless enough to say, "This is out of my area of expertise. I can help in some ways, but you need to see someone else who specializes in this." For example, David has a basic understanding of the different style markers of the various pop/rock genres, but gladly sends his clients to Sheri Sanders, who wrote *Rock the Audition*. She's a phenomenal resource (and can be found at rock-the-audition.com).

Students respect teachers who are honest about their boundaries. We don't have to be an expert on everything - we simply have to build our network and know where to send students for the information they need to succeed.

In short, share your knowledge, connect them to other resources, and read on. We have lots of great information for you!

## PARENT

You have a budding musical theatre performer in your home? Congratulations! They've told you by now they want to go to college for musical theatre. If you're reading this book, chances are you're supportive of their dream, or are at least willing to hear them out. That's a great start. Your child is one of the lucky ones. But how do you know if pursuing a college degree in musical theatre is the right path for your child?

Many parents worry about their children going into any arts profession for fear they won't be able to support themselves. It's a valid fear. A large part of being a performing artist is figuring out how to actually make a living. Many performers have "survival jobs" so they can audition and study until they get hired (and many times even after that). Auditioning is a grueling process laced with rejection. It takes thick skin and a lot of grit to be patient and keep showing up. Most theatre jobs are, by nature, short term, meaning actors are constantly job hunting and identifying creative ways to supplement their income. An actor needs to be a great performer, skilled networker, entrepreneur, and a marketing guru.

The reality TV show phenomenon has created a culture of people who believe they can become a star in a day. The *actual* reality is that it takes years of study to be prepared when an opportunity appears. If success is being in the right place at the right time, it's the performer's job to be ready.

The best thing you can do to determine if your child is serious about being a professional performer is get them proper training before they go to college. This will both prepare them for college auditions and give them a better perspective of all that's involved in being a  successful performing artist.

A good college musical theatre training program will ensure your child has the necessary skills to tackle the challenges they will face as a budding performing artist. They will take classes in voice, scene study, dance, speech/diction, theatre history, auditioning, sight singing, stage combat, theatre craft, and more. It's a rigorous schedule, so it's important you let your child know college musical theatre programs are much more than "putting on shows." The workload for a musical theatre performer is just as challenging - if not more than - other bachelors programs. Many programs don't allow Freshmen to perform because they're busy doing important foundational training.

Your child's decision to pursue musical theatre will cost you a lot of money, but more than that, it will consume a large chunk of your time. You will need to help them find good teachers to prepare for auditions; take them to/from their lessons, classes, summer intensives, and campus visits; help research the best colleges, universities, or conservatories for them; and keep them organized, balancing all the paperwork, requirements, and deadlines that come their way.

There will be many spinning plates, especially when college audition season begins (as early as November). You will most likely need to take time off work to travel with your child to prospective schools or regional audition sites. You might be on the road almost every weekend for up to 8 weeks at the height of audition season. Once your child is accepted and makes a decision on where to attend, you'll want to help them look for scholarships and other financial aid support. All this in addition to your current hectic life.

The decision to go to college is a big investment for any family, but especially for that of the musical theatre student. Your complete involvement is mandatory for them to be successful. Investing in your child this way will not only be a clear sign how much you love and support them, it will give you a full sense of how to navigate the challenges that will arise along the way.

Sit down with your child and have a talk about these realities. Ask them why they want to study musical theatre. Ask them what they think it will be like. Ask if there's anything else they can see themselves doing. Ask if they're willing to work at something else while pursuing their dream of being a working performer.

Here are some qualities your child must have to be successful in college and the musical theatre industry:

- Strong organizational and time management skills
- An ability to receive criticism and not take it personally
- Works well under pressure
- An ability to multi-task or toggle back and forth between tasks

If you think your child is serious enough and has the tenacity to be a successful musical theatre performer, by all means support them. There are many ways to make a successful career as a performer and most of them aren't on Broadway. With the skills they'll learn, they will be more than ready to adapt and achieve in their academic and professional careers.

# CHAPTER 2: HOW DO I KNOW WHICH PROGRAM IS RIGHT FOR ME?

You've turned the page! That means we didn't scare you away with the previous chapter. Now the tough work of researching and choosing a musical theatre program begins. So how do you know if a particular musical theatre program will be a good fit for you?

This is a very important (not to mention expensive) question. There are literally hundreds of musical theatre programs in the United States and internationally. Some programs are two years and some are four. You can graduate with a Bachelor of Arts, a Bachelor of Fine Arts, a Bachelor of Music, or earn a certificate. What might be the right training for one person might be completely inappropriate for another.

Would you believe many people don't give this much thought? We're fairly smart folks, but even we didn't necessarily choose our institutions for the "right reasons." Laura chose NYU because it was in the heart of New York City, but ended up loving the program. David wanted to study with a famous teacher in grad school, but ended up getting assigned to a different studio that ended up being better for him. We got lucky, that's for sure. But we want you to be better informed than we were.

Ideally, you'll make the right decision straight out of the gate. However, would it shock you to know that lots of college students transfer from program to program in the hopes of being happier with their education? Every program is built differently and has different requirements. This means credits might not transfer and you may have to spend more money to get the education you desire.

Why is it so hard to make this decision? Because there are endless variations in musical theatre programs, all of which need to be deciphered and weighed against each other, along with logistical considerations (i.e. how close/far is it from home? is it in a city? how are the institution's facilities? how much is the tuition? what

15

are the scholarship and financial aid opportunities?). Beyond these detailed decisions, you must also be able to look at the larger picture and ask: "How will this school help me become a working musical theatre professional?"

Considering that the average four-year musical theatre degree will cost upwards of $200,000 or more (yes, everyone let that sink in for a second), we want you to make smart decisions now. Rather than recommending certain programs over others, we're going to give you several points to consider as you think about where you could imagine spending the next two to four years.

**Degree Programs**

There's an age-old question: conservatory or liberal arts? Diehard musical theatre students may be hungry to dive into a conservatory program. Parents may be more inclined to have their children get a liberal arts degree. Which is better?

There's no way to answer this for you. All programs are built differently, regardless of how many credits are available in your area of concentration.

To help you get started, we've created the below chart comparing credits between a conservatory program (Shenandoah Conservatory, BFA Musical Theatre) and a liberal arts program (Syracuse University, BFA).

| Conservatory | | Liberal Arts | |
|---|---|---|---|
| Drama Requirements | 40 | Drama Requirements | 37 |
| Musical Theatre Requirements | 16 | Musical Theatre Requirements | 20 |
| Dance Requirements | 12 | Dance Requirements | 18 |
| Applied Music Requirements | 39 | Applied Music Requirements | 14 |
| Drama Electives | 3 | Drama Electives | 9 |
| Academic Requirements & Electives | 15 | Academic Requirements & Electives | 30 |
| **Total Credits** | **125** | **Total Credits** | **128** |

Again, keep in mind each program is its own world with a different amount of credits assigned to various parts of the curriculum. What we want you to pay attention to right now is the "Academic Requirements & Electives" section. When compared with the liberal arts institution, the conservatory calls for only half the amount of "Gen Ed" (general education) requirements and electives. This means you will be focusing more on your area of study in a conservatory setting.

Benefits & Challenges of Conservatory Training

The term conservatory does not denote any one specific type of training. Programs vary wildly with some being part of a college or university, offering Bachelor of Fine Arts degrees, while others are stand-alone schools issuing degrees or certificates. Some conservatories focus on specialized training techniques while others offer the same well-rounded training you will find at a college or university.

The one thing all conservatory programs have in common is a focus on performing. So if you are just looking to hone your performance skills with little academic training, the conservatory route may work for you. If you choose a certificate program, they are often only two years instead of four, which may cost less - another benefit.

But keep in mind, these benefits might also present themselves as challenges. Remember what we said in the previous chapter: this course of study is grueling. Having little to no escape from it can be a challenge.

Intense artistic training with little to no outside academic classes could be an issue later if you choose to apply to graduate school. And many times, musical theatre students end up doing something other than their exact area of study. Focusing solely on performance can be limiting when those vocations become more viable options.

# Benefits & Challenges of Liberal Arts Training

There are many benefits to a liberal arts education (full disclosure: that's our educational background). As Kevin Connell, Recruiter for Marymount Manhattan College's Theatre Arts Program, says: "Theatre isn't about theatre. It's about history, philosophy, psychology, even math." It's wiser to a be a well-rounded actor with knowledge in many areas. In most liberal arts programs, you can tailor your general education courses to subjects that are directly applicable to your work as an actor. In our estimation, history, philosophy, and psychology are a must.

Today's marketplace demands the musical theatre professional have a diverse portfolio of gifts. You might realize halfway through your program that you have an interest in business. If you were at a conservatory, your options might be limited. You have much more flexibility to discover who you are in a liberal arts program. And that's important because, as we previously mentioned, who you are and what you want are subject to change during your undergraduate degree. Those friends of ours who became lawyers or doctors? They may have only needed a couple extra courses before moving on to their area of specialty. Here are some of the vocations our former students are now successfully pursuing:

- Children's Entertainer
- Chef
- Chiropractor
- DJ
- Elementary Music Teacher
- ESL (English as a Second Language) Instructor
- Hairdresser
- Interior Designer
- Massage Therapist
- Photographer
- Real Estate Agent
- Talent Agent
- Web Designer

And certainly, many of our former students are pursuing musical theatre as well, but they have other skills that help round out their income. Again, a liberal arts degree will open doors to those possibilities.

In the challenges column, a four-year musical theatre degree is expensive with little chance of paying back any student loans your first few years out of school. And while taking extensive general education classes will expand your worldview, that does mean you will be doing your calculus homework along with your theatre history homework.

## BA, BFA, or BM?

You'll also need to decide what kind of degree you want to pursue. This means you need to know the difference between a BA (Bachelor of Arts), BFA (Bachelor of Fine Arts), and BM (Bachelor of Music). Sometimes it's the amount of coursework focused on the performing arts. Generally, BA students are required to take more classes outside their major, while the BFA and BM students take more classes focused on their field of study. In some programs, the difference between a BA and BFA might be commercial versus classical training (i.e., Acting for the Camera versus Shakespeare and Chekhov). Some BFA programs are born out of liberal arts institutions, while others are obtained through conservatories.

Having said all this, the kind of degree is less important than its substance. For example, some folks might tell you a BFA is the better degree. Not true. Every program is designed differently. It's all in how it's packaged. The BFA program at one institution might be quite similar to the BA program at another. The "F" does not make the degree or training better.

It's also important to ensure your training is balanced. Bachelor of Music programs have (not surprisingly) a greater emphasis on music training, including: music theory, sight-singing, and music history. This kind of training can really help your musicianship, but be sure to look at the course offerings closely. When one concentration is emphasized, another will naturally have fewer classes. With every program, you should note how many acting, dancing, and voice training classes are offered.

Many musical theatre programs list their core curriculums online. Visit the musical theatre department website and print out the course requirements to compare them. Differences will become very apparent when you look at them in this way. This will give you a clear indication of the education you'll be receiving.

No undergraduate program can do everything. While four years is a long time, there will be skills you won't have time to learn. You can supplement with internships, summer programs, and graduate school. Being a musical theatre performer means a lifetime of learning. Choose a strong foundation on which to build.

## Certificate Programs

Another training option is a non-degree certificate program. Certificate programs are typically one- to two-year programs housed in a stand-alone school that may call itself a conservatory, an academy, or simply a school. The training is exclusively based in the performing arts with little to no academics. The biggest difference between a certificate program and a degree program is that you may not receive college credits for your classes and the program does not culminate in a degree. You receive a Certificate of Completion at the end of the program.

Benefits to a certificate program: they usually cost less than a college program, and only take one to two years to complete, and you will not have to take any academic classes. But if you begin a certificate program and decide you want to transfer to a college and pursue a degree, you may not get credit for the classes you've taken and will have to start over.

We fully acknowledge everyone needs something different. You may decide to diversify and apply to some conservatories and liberal arts schools, or BFA, BM, BA, and certificate programs. This will give you the opportunity to compare the different programs. Just be sure to investigate the course content in each of your programs of interest. This will help you define which program is right for you.

## Other Considerations

Every degree program should have a clear philosophy about the education they provide and how it prepares musical theatre performers for success in a competitive industry. Institutions should also be able to clearly explain how their program is changing with the industry. What musical theatre performers needed to know five years ago is now obsolete. The industry is quickly changing, and it's important the institutions you're applying to are both aware of these changes and meeting those demands with solid training.

Some programs will have a jury process at the end of the Sophomore year to review whether or not the student should continue in the program. Others don't cut students. You want to make sure to understand the differences and how that might affect your trajectory as a performer.

In Chapter 9 will offer some questions to consider when you visit the institutions, but we recommend you research how each program will prepare you for a career. Consider the whole musical theatre program and evaluate everything from their philosophy about training to their connection to the industry. A good program should balance training, business skills, as well as awareness of current industry demands. Looking at a school's website is a great place to start. The musical theatre program's homepage will often have a "mission statement" containing their point of view on training. They may also talk about performance opportunities and their faculty. While not always a totally honest view of a program (it's written by marketing people, after all), it should give you some idea where the program focuses their energy. Once you have collected information from a few schools and placed them side by side, you will begin to see some real differences and be able to start to making choices about which programs appeal to you.

## "We Graduated Famous People!"

Most every college or university has a success story. Others have a strong track record of producing what we would consider musical theatre "stars." ***Please do not choose a school based on this.*** Just because Angelica Magillicutty is famous doesn't mean you will be. As we said, success is talent and skill finding the right opportunity at the right moment. That can happen to almost anyone, almost anywhere. There are plenty of very talented people who aren't successful (in the way we often would define success, which is a conundrum in and of itself...). Is the performer's training solely to blame?

We bristle when schools (and teachers) take credit for someone else's success. It's certainly OK to be proud of an alumnus, but the institution didn't do the audition that got the performer the job. We both have students and clients who have gone on to great things. We're honored to have been helpful to them. If they feel called to sing our praises, wonderful. We don't teach for the praise. The same should be true of the institutions where you apply.

Focusing on who graduated where is limiting. After all, this is about _you_.

## What Else Should You Be Looking For in a Program?

Here's a short list of some other things to consider when looking at musical theatre programs:

- **Learn about the faculty.** See who the current faculty are and read their bios. Are they diverse in age, gender, race, sexual identity, and experience? This is vitally important for a well-rounded education. Most of this information should be found on the theatre department's website. You should be looking for the same diversity in the student body.
- **Visit a classroom.** You should ask to sit in on a couple of classes if you're visiting the institution prior to your audition day. You want to get a sense of how the teachers

inspire their students to grow as performing artists. You will get a sense of whether or not a particular teacher or program is right for you based on what you see. Note that some programs only allow prospective students to sit in on a class. Sorry parents!

- **Talk to students who attend the institution.** The best way to put your finger on the pulse of a school is by talking to the students. Ask them what they like about the program and what they find challenging. Every program is going to have its strengths and weaknesses. Students will have a unique perspective on this. Of course, you may have to take some of this feedback with a grain of salt. Pair this information with your own experiences for a more well-rounded perspective.

- **Attend a production.** An institution's productions are essentially a calling card for their program. If possible, attend a production and take note not only of the performances, but the facility, technical elements, and community response. This will tell you more about how the program functions in the context of the broader institution. If you're unable to attend a production, research past performances on YouTube.

- **How many performing opportunities are there per semester? per year?** You'll want to apply the skills you learn in your lessons and classes to a fully produced show. Some programs only produce one musical a year, making the competition very stiff when it comes to casting. Some programs don't allow Freshmen to perform. Call the theatre office if this information is not readily available or unclear. If there is a graduate program in the department, ask if undergraduates and graduates audition together for casting in mainstage shows.

- **How is the institution coping with the ever-changing industry?** When we first came to New York, musical theatre performers only needed about five songs in their audition book. Today, audition books must contain about 20 songs in a wide variety of styles. Performers should have audition cuts of contemporary musical theatre and pop/rock genres (up-tempos and ballads from each decade, starting with the 1950's) and understand how to sing in each of those musical idioms in a way that still incorporates a healthy technique. Some programs haven't yet caught up with the changing tide of the industry. Make sure the programs you're considering understand how to produce versatile performers.

- **How will AP (Advance Placement) credits be applied to your required coursework?** Often times students will enter college with upwards of 15 or more AP credits, which can be applied to coursework required for the degree. Ask how your credits will be applied to maximize your time (and money).

- **What are the facilities like (practice rooms, theatres, dorms, etc...)?** You're going to be spending many hours in these rooms (especially the practice rooms), preparing for lessons and classes. Make sure they are places you'd like to work. If the school doesn't put their money toward maintaining their facilities, that says something about their investment in the musical theatre program.

- **How many students are in the program?** A larger program may offer more performance opportunities but it may also be easier to get lost in the crowd. Is it important to attend a school where you're more likely to get individualized attention?

- **Are there theatrical internships or performance opportunities?** What professional theaters are close to the college? Is there an easy way to reach them using public transportation or do they require driving? Have current or former students regularly performed there? Does the college have strong relationships with these theaters?

- **What is the history and future outlook of the program?** Some musical theatre programs have long-standing traditions of excellence and are well regarded in the industry. They are housed in an institution that supports them and their leadership is stable. Other programs may have recently lost strong leadership, thus becoming less of a priority in the institution's eyes. Still other programs seem to only be gaining momentum, attracting the best faculty, showing signs of investment by the college, etc...

24

Every program goes through this kind of ebb and flow. Determining where a program is in their cycle requires a bit of detective work. Again, speaking to students and faculty about the institution's commitment to the program can be helpful.

- **What kind of support system is available for students?** College is hard. Most every student goes through a period of struggle, either academically, emotionally, or both. Find out how the college or university supports their students through counseling and other on-campus communities.

You can decide for yourself which of these things is more important. You might find that, while you love a program, their facilities are not the best. The question is: can you deal with that for two to four years?

While there's a lot of information to collect and balance, we also recommend you go with your gut. If you get a good feeling about a program after researching and talking to people associated with it, consider applying. When you compare the programs you choose in the following months, you'll better be able to discern which one is right for you.

Doing your research online will help narrow down your choices and target the programs that best fit your requirements. Then consider making a balanced list of top choices, schools you're interested in, and some safety schools. You'll want to have a couple from each category on your list, given that competition has become incredibly stiff for these programs. You might want to consider applying to about 12 to 15 schools and take it from there. We believe anything more than that is going to be spreading yourself too thin.

Look at **Appendix A** for an example of a chart you can create to easily compare all the different criteria you might have for a musical theatre program. We also recommend creating a binder with tabs for each school. In each section, you can keep specific details on the institution that might not fit in the chart, along with any paperwork you receive along the way (correspondences, audition day details, itineraries, hotel confirmations, notes on visits, etc…). This will become highly valuable when auditioning at the various schools and especially when deciding where to attend.

## STUDENT

We realize this is a lot of information and understand if you're feeling overwhelmed. It would be easier to just say, "I like the way the campus looks" or "my best friend's sister goes there," send in your application, and hope for the best. Hopefully you have a parent or teacher who can help you navigate this process. But even if you're on you're own, you can do this. Doing the research to pick the right program is worth your time. The competition to be a working professional artist is fierce. The better trained you are, the better your chances will be for success.

And this is a decision you have to make for yourself. Just because you know someone at a specific program and they like it doesn't mean it's the right program for you. One of our former students attended a university with a prominent musical theatre program in New York City his Freshman year because several of his friends were there. After a year, he decided it wasn't for him, and ended up transferring. It wasn't a wasted year, per se, but the new program was a better fit for him.

Everyone learns differently. Everyone has different strengths. And everyone has different tastes. We're sure there's been a teacher in your high school you really loved that your friends may have disliked. Why was that? Were they not prepared in class? Were you more interested in the subject? There may be many different reasons. You have to figure out what those differences are know why the teacher works for you. Similarly, you need to discern which program will help you be the best artist you can be.

So, how specifically do you do that? First, if you have teachers whom you trust and know your work, ask them what programs they think might be strong options for you based on your strengths and weaknesses. Ask your guidance counselor for help in researching institutions with strong musical theatre schools. Share this book with them so they have a better sense of what will be required of you and how they can help. And, because you're a child of the 21st Century, you know how to use the internet to your advantage. Research the different programs that inspire you and start comparing them to each other.

Avoid chat rooms, which may provide more opinions than facts. Also avoid articles that promote a particular school because of their alumni (we're purposely repeating this because we see so many students duped into auditioning at certain schools because of the caché, not because of the training). At the end of the day, it's going to be up to you to weigh all the information you receive. Make sure you're considering credible sources.

## TEACHER

This is where your research, deduction, and oral skills will be put to the test. Credits and program differences are not the most engaging topics, but it's important you help the young artist understand the differences in the education they'll receive at the institutions they're looking at.

Consider creating a chart of the different programs, their requirements (audition and otherwise), deadlines and a brief outline of their curriculums (**See Appendix A** for a sample). This will make it much easier to decide what's best for all involved. Plus, it will help everyone maintain a more discerning eye when institutions begin selling their programs (it is a business, after all). Data will help balance out that sleek new theatre a college has or the warm fuzzies one might get when visiting another campus. Hopefully the young artists will get those things too, but in conjunction with a strong degree program.

Sometimes it's hard to be objective about a program. We've both wanted to "guide' a student to or away from a particular institution because of our own experiences. In these moments, we try to step back and remind ourselves we're not the ones attending college. Keep an open mind and offer advice when requested. This will encourage the student to develop their own ideas about the schools they're interested in.

## PARENT

Balancing your child's wants with your family's financial considerations is a big part of choosing a college. Helping them narrow down the kind of training they want and need is a good way to start. Unless you have a real Type A kid, you will need to be the driver of this part of the process as well as the organizer for all this information. If you can, ask a teacher or guidance counselor to help you start a list of possible schools. Then print out curricula and begin comparing the degrees and classes offered. As much as you may have a preference, avoid recommending one school over another at this point. Consider creating a chart of the different programs, their requirements (audition and otherwise), deadlines and a brief outline of their curriculums (**See Appendix A** for a sample). Talk with your child about the benefits and challenges of each program. Things will be become clearer once you are able to compare programs based on their content versus their slick website or brochure.

There are so many questions that precede how you will help your young artist pay for college. While it might be challenging, we recommend being open to all possibilities and crossing the bridge of how to pay for the education as you help your child narrow down their options. We have resources to help you out in Chapter 9.

That's not to say you should ignore the financial realities all together. Hopefully, you've been able to plan for this eventuality, but we also recognize many families are just keeping their heads above water. In our opinion, there's always a way to help your child succeed. Some state schools have wonderful musical theatre programs at literally a third of the price. It might be better for your child to start at a junior college to get most of their "Gen Ed" courses out of the way more cost effectively. You can start researching scholarship and financial aid during their sophomore or junior year. Money is only one of many cogs in the process of choosing the best musical theatre program for them.

# CHAPTER 3: WHEN SHOULD I START PREPARING FOR MY AUDITIONS?

It happens every audition season. Eager students come see us to prepare for a performing arts high school or college audition they have in only a few weeks. They have not picked out their material or done any research on the institution. They might not even know what the audition requirements are. They just know they want to audition.

While we applaud the desire to audition, this is an almost impossible situation for teachers and coaches. In order to effectively prepare for an audition, the process of picking out material and practicing should have begun months ago. It takes time to help someone get their voice aligned and pick out appropriate song repertoire for the auditions (especially if they're doing several), as many schools have very specific requirements. Anything else is just a quick band-aid with a lick-and-a-promise hope that what we work on will translate to the audition.

The same is true with monologue auditions. It's important to understand how to find a good monologue; cut it to be sure it has a strong beginning, middle, and end; and then practice it.

Dance will also be part of the audition process. This is the piece of the puzzle most people forget about (or completely ignore), to their detriment. Being able to communicate an idea through movement takes time, especially when there are several different genres of dance to know.

We'll break down each of these more later in the chapter.

And then there's the daunting task of the audition itself. Most likely, this will be one of your first experiences auditioning at this level and intensity. Not to trivialize auditions for high school musicals and summer intensives, but auditioning for college musical theatre programs takes a tremendous amount of knowledge and finesse. Even those young artists with significant experience as a performer will find college auditions a completely different beast because each program has its own requirements and approach. This means you must know your audition material well enough to be flexible in each audition environment.

Given this, we recommend the student begin preparing for college auditions the summer between their junior and senior year. If the student has not yet begun studying voice, drama, or dance, it is better for them to start the summer between the sophomore and junior year.

If you're reading this and thinking, "Oh no! I'm behind!" don't panic. You may be able to catch up with the help of a good audition coach, who should be able to help pick and prepare audition material. If you're having trouble finding a coach, ask your high school drama or music teacher for a recommendation.

The more you can work ahead, the better.

**A Word of Warning:** There will be college audition coaches or companies who will promise you your choice of top schools because of their connections and "fool-proof" tips. They will request hundreds of dollars (maybe $500-$1,000) for their services and will explain they're doing a lot of the leg work for you. They might tell you they've helped tons of students get into the best musical theatre programs and can do the same for you.

In addition to charging you, they will also charge an institution a similar amount, most all of which goes directly into their pocket. Say they take on 100 students and 20-30 colleges. That's a darn good annual salary when it all adds up, wouldn't you say?

Do not work with such a person or company. While it's good to have resources, anyone who suggests they can essentially broker a deal in your favor is either lying, or using their connections in an unprofessional way.

Also, if you, as a collective team, don't have the fortitude to do the work required to get into a musical theatre program, how will the student be able to muster the strength needed to complete such an intense degree? While we recognize applying to and auditioning for musical theatre programs can be very time-consuming, it in no way matches the challenging work that lies ahead. Do this hard-won work and, as is true with good training, you will be rewarded with knowledge and perspective.

This isn't to say you need to do all this by yourself. Of course not. You'll have lots of people to help you. But when it comes to auditioning for college, no one resource is going to do everything for you. Even this book, which we've written using our experience, passion, and considerable research, won't speak to everything you need to know. How could it? An audition is a highly individual experience. No one has all the answers.

There are no shortcuts. But if you all plan ahead, know exactly why you're applying to specific schools, and get the right pre-college training, you will remain in the driver's seat of this challenging and exciting ride.

Pre-College Training

Some students you encounter during the audition process will have started training for a performance career as early as elementary or middle school. Many students attend performing arts high schools. There are even performing arts middle schools now!

Does this lack of exposure spell disaster for the student without similar experiences? Not necessarily. It's wonderful when natural aptitudes are discovered and fostered early. And yet, training at an early age can sometimes create problems later on. Not all training is good training.

What does good training look like? It should meet the following requirements:

- Allows the young artist more expressive freedom through a healthy technique. Great acting, singing, and dancing should be free from tension.

- Encourages and celebrates individuality. The teacher should be able to pinpoint what the young artist does well or what makes them unique and how to use that to their benefit.
- Places the work a student is doing in a broader context. Teachers should have an extensive knowledge of current industry demands and be able to tell a student how they might fit into it.

Some of you will find this kind of training rather easily, especially if you're in a major city. Others of you will need to search for the right teachers to help you. As we said in the first chapter, researching and working with the right teachers will take time and discipline. For some, traveling to the nearest metropolitan area, having a lesson, and returning home will take up to 5 hours out of their day. You can, however, connect with teachers in other ways. For example, we both teach via Skype (you can reach Laura at **ljosepher** and David at **siscosongs**). Think outside the box and make sure you have the best support going into this process.

Summer Intensives

Summer intensives are a wonderful way to get a full understanding of what is demanded of the musical theatre performer while also receiving the training needed to succeed at college auditions. Not only can young artists discover whether or not they thrive in this kind of immersive environment, it might also help clarify which is better for them: a liberal arts education or conservatory training.

There are as many kinds of summer intensives as there are higher education institutions. In fact, you'll find that many musical theatre programs have summer institutes, which might be a great way to explore the school. Intensives usually range from 1-8 weeks and often cover several areas of study: dance, voice, acting, improv, scene study, etc... You don't need to go to the most expensive or exclusive summer program to get something valuable out of the experience. Research the teachers of the programs, just as you would the schools you're interested in. Get a sense of their experience in the industry and how they might be able to help you.

If you have personal areas of weakness (i.e. dance, sight singing, vocal technique, etc...), look for a summer intensive that will speak to those weaknesses.

For the last five years, David has been the musical director and vocal coach for a two-week summer intensive. His loves watching the students connect the dots between the work they're asked to do as singers, actors, and dancers. Often times a student will say, "That's so weird you talked about my breath, because my acting teacher just told me I was holding my breath in my scene." Intensives are a great way to begin to see the whole picture and experience how addressing an issue in one medium might free you up in another.

Even if you attend a performing arts high school, we recommend a summer intensive. At the very least, it will expand your horizons and help provide you with a better perspective on your upcoming college auditions.

If this kind of experience is too expensive for you, look into other opportunities at the local, county, and state level. Many states have summer arts programs that are much less expensive. Summer stock and arts camps can also provide great experiences. The idea is to make sure you have a portfolio of different experiences prior to auditioning for college. All of them will positively inform your audition process.

See **Appendix B** for a list of summer intensives in the United States.

Working Ahead

There are a couple things that will get you ahead of the game, beyond good training. They include:

- **Get new headshots.** Most schools will ask you to submit a headshot and resume on your audition day. It's important to note that senior pictures and headshots are completely different things. Headshots should meet very specific demands, most importantly reflecting the performer's current look. Check out articles on backstage.com (i.e. "4 Tips for Finding the Right Headshot Photographer") and other sites to find out more about choosing a good photographer and great headshot.

- **Develop a resume.** This is an important one-page document, which will most definitely be looked at when institutions are weighing whether or not you're a match for them. Start this early with the help of your guidance counselor. Again, look to online resources like resume-templates.com/acting/ to get some ideas on how to create the proper look for your resume. Put your name bold and centered at the top and list your personal stats (height, hair and eye color, vocal range, etc...). Don't list personal information such as address or social security number, but do include a phone number and email address. Don't worry if you don't have a lot of experience yet. List shows you've done, awards you have won, and any special skills. Include any classes you've taken and teachers you've studied with. If you've only done scene work in an acting class, put that on there. And if you have extra space, insert a small photo (2" x 3") at the top right to help the adjudicators identify you.

- **Draft your college essay.** It is incredibly challenging to stand out in a college essay. Just think of how many of them admissions people read in a year. Are they really reading anything new? You have to find a way to differentiate yourself from others applying to the same institution, and that takes time. Begin working on this before you even start the application process. Check out suggestions from the Princeton Review and other resources your guidance counselor can provide on writing a strong essay. You'll most likely need to adjust each essay to the specific institution, but at least you won't be inundated with deadlines.

- **Obtain letters of recommendation.** Start thinking about who you'd like to have write your letter(s) of recommendation. Many times, this gets left to the last-minute, which results in hastily-written letters that may not represent you in the best light. Planning ahead will help you get a better response from your teacher(s).

## STUDENT

Let's get specific about why auditioning for college musical theatre programs requires months of preparation.

To state the obvious: you have to sing, dance _and_ act well. Students that come to us at the last-minute to "cram" before their musical theatre auditions either end up giving good technical performances with no interpretation, or unfocused performances that don't illuminate who they are as young artists. The same is true of dance: students who are not comfortable in their body are overly concerned with doing a combination "right" rather than being expressive. Either way, these students aren't usually successful in getting into their desired program.

Here's a breakdown of what you need to know for each of the areas of study in musical theatre.

Voice

You will most likely need a Golden Age up-tempo and ballad, contemporary musical theatre song, and possibly a pop/rock song for your musical theatre auditions. Those auditioning for BM programs will probably need to prepare an art song (sometimes in English or another language). If you're a young woman and sing in both legit and belt voice, you may have the opportunity to sing two songs that showcase those styles of singing (which is different than the genre classifications listed above). Either way, you'll need to coordinate which songs meet the audition requirements for each program. Look at the spreadsheet you created (see **Appendix A**) to see where there might be overlap. Ask your teachers and coaches for help.

It may take you at least 3 to 4 weeks for you to learn and fully incorporate a new song into your technique. After you've learned it, you'll then need to find the acting beats and incorporate them into the technical work you've done. We'll discuss this in Chapter 4.

As we mentioned earlier, if you've been studying voice on a regular basis, you should consider picking out your audition repertoire the summer between your junior and senior year. This gives you plenty of time to take the songs apart and be prepared for your auditions, which could fall as early as the first weekend in November.

If you haven't been studying voice on a regular basis, start now. It would be smart to make sure you have at least a year of technique under your belt before you pick repertoire for your auditions. That means starting the summer between your sophomore and junior year.

Regardless of how long you've been studying, make sure you're working with a voice teacher who really understands vocal technique and the demands of musical theatre. It's not the same thing as classical singing, though many of the technical approaches may be similar.

A good voice teacher should be able to help you pick out appropriate repertoire for auditions and teach you how to sing with consistent ease in all different styles of music (i.e. legit, belt, Golden Age, contemporary, pop/rock, etc…).

Finding the right voice teacher is a very personal thing. If you're not feeling "the vibe" with a teacher, keep looking. Similarly, if the teacher is having you do something that makes you feel uncomfortable, vocally or otherwise, move on. You have a lot to learn and no time to waste. There are plenty of good teachers out there who will be able to help you accomplish all you're setting out to do.

Drama

You will most likely need a contemporary and classical (Shakespeare, etc…) monologue for your auditions, depending on the program. It's best to find a couple different options for each genre and prepare them all. You can decide which one you'd like to perform as the audition gets closer.

Preparing for an audition is different than learning a role for your school production. If you've never taken an acting class, your junior year is a great time to start.

Why take a class? You will learn skills like how to create character and analyze text. You will be exposed to new material and work with different people. You will have to stand in front of the class and present each week. All of these skills will help you prepare for your college auditions.

How do you pick an acting class? If there are several classes to choose from in your town, ask to sit in on them. Just because a teacher has a great reputation doesn't mean they're the best teacher for you. Acting is a very personal craft and you should feel safe and comfortable in the class you choose. While the in-depth work may at times feel uncomfortable, you should never feel attacked or unsafe.

There are many styles and techniques of acting: Stanislavski's "the Method;" the Atlantic Technique's Practical Aesthetics; Meisner Technique, just to name a few. Most actors wind up incorporating several techniques into their work. The key is finding a teacher you like and a technique that makes sense to you.

Don't feel you have to be in a "teen" class. Many adult classes can be fine, as long as they are aimed at your experience level, the teacher is respectful of your age and maturity, and he or she will help you pick appropriate material. Ideally, you should take an acting class for 6-12 months before picking out audition material for your college auditions.

Dance

There are just as many things to know about giving a successful dance audition as there are about giving strong song or monologue auditions. For this reason, it's important to start dance classes between your sophomore and junior year if you haven't previously had experience.

Every college runs their dance auditions differently. For some, you'll do a combination. For others, you will be adjudicated on several different styles of dance.

We asked Rusty Curcio, who administers the dance auditions for the musical theatre program at Wagner College, what you need to know. He suggested novice students take good ballet and classical jazz classes. In order to have the physical tone and strength you need going into a dance audition, you should attend dance class three times a week. That breaks down to 2 ballet and/or classical jazz and another dance class that's fun and original.

Only you can know how comfortable you are with your body and how naturally dance comes to you. If it's a real challenge, start earlier rather than later. Rusty said Wagner College is looking for confident dancers who are able to absorb adjustments and know proper etiquette. This includes things like having the right dance attire and shoes, taking off jewelry and watches, pulling hair back from your face (if applicable), and moving quickly when you're asked.

Rusty also mentioned it's not uncommon for him to throw a seasoned dancer a curveball to see if they can move beyond technique and create an artistic choice. It's important you show you're open and available to learn, not just show what you know. Your dance audition may be the most collaborative portion of your audition day. Take advantage of that by listening and making strong choices.

Where should you take dance classes? If you have a regional ballet company, start there. Research dance studios in your area. Take a summer intensive that heavily features a dance component. Any combination of these things will help you get the technical foundation you need.

*Remember that dance is a physical expression of a dramatic action.* Invest the time necessary to develop a solid technique, which will allow you to make artistic choices while learning a new combination.

But just dancing well isn't enough. It's important to think of all of your training cumulatively. Schools don't want to see just that you can dance, and sing, and act. They want to see how you put those skills together. Are you telling a story while you dance? Does your song show a strong character? How do you use your body during your monologue? One of our students shared with us that she wishes she would've known just how important the acting side of an audition is. Her instinct was to go in and belt as loud and high as possible, and acting became secondary. Finding a song to show off your voice is important, but equally it's important to showcase your ability to understand and portray a character. Keep this in mind as you begin your training and seek out teachers who can help you integrate all the skills you're learning.

## TEACHER

We hope you agree it's incredibly important that young artists receive training from teachers who have a solid technical background and understand the demands of today's musical theatre industry. It is not uncommon for students to come into auditions unprepared for the realities of the day. Unhealthy technique, improper repertoire choices, or a poor audition cut can stand in the way of a student being accepted to a musical theatre program.

Sometimes we have the skill sets to help the young artist and other times we have an opportunity to put them in touch with someone who will be able to help them more than we could. That's part of the selflessness that comes with being a teacher.

Beyond helping the student develop a solid technique, you can keep them focused by taking the following steps:
- Ask them where they plan to audition
- Ask them what the audition requirements are for each school

41

- Develop a timetable of when to prepare the material

It's important they give themselves (and you, of course, as you'll be helping them) plenty of time to find repertoire that meets the various audition criteria for the several schools. You will be instrumental in this process and we have some great resources for you later on in the book.

## PARENT

As we said at the beginning of the chapter, it's important your child start taking voice lessons, acting classes, and dance classes during their sophomore year to be competitive. We realize this will get expensive fast. Give them as much exposure as you can afford. Sometimes summer intensives are the best bet because everything is available to the student in one place. Use your judgment and ask your child's guidance counselor what resources they might have to support your child.

In this phase of the audition process, you will need to help coordinate between your child and their teachers, making sure everyone is on the same page. Every musical theatre program has slightly different audition requirements. While some will overlap, it's important your child have a clear understanding of what they need to prepare for auditions and how long it will take to truly get each piece into their body (which is longer than they think). Make sure their teachers have a game plan in place and help them understand how (and how long) to practice so they make good headway.

The other thing you'll want to consider during this time is the order in which your child will audition at their chosen programs. In the first chapter, we mentioned that, depending on how many programs they're auditioning for, it's quite likely you could be traveling most every weekend from January to early March. Some schools start auditions as early as November and others have early decision days. It's important to look at the audition schedules and start mapping out the logistics of traveling to the various schools.

It's also imperative you and your child sit down and consider which programs are most important to them, as this will also play into the audition dates you select. It might be smart to put what might be considered a "safety school" first so your child essentially has a dress rehearsal for the other auditions. Other schools that seem very competitive might go in the middle of the audition season, so as the student receives acceptance or rejection letters, the game plan can be amended.

Of course, many programs won't allow you to select an audition date until the student's application has been completed and accepted. This requires many steps as well, and it behooves everyone to be on top of any missing paperwork so it doesn't negatively impact audition date choices.

Did you ever dream this could be so complicated?!

After you've done all this, you need to do the toughest thing of all: step back. Even (and especially) if you have experience as a singer, teacher, or performer, you need to let your child prepare in their own way. Ask them how you can best support them. Ask if they want to talk about how they're doing or feeling. Ask if they feel prepared. Remind them you're there if they need you. Then give them space.

# CHAPTER 4: HOW DO I CHOOSE MATERIAL?

A couple of years ago, while sitting through a particularly long day of auditions, a young girl announced she would be singing "Bring Him Home" from *Les Misérables*. Slight problem with that: she was not a 40- to 50-year-old white man. Needless to say, the song was completely inappropriate for her.

We see this so often in auditions: students choose material that doesn't match their age, sexual identity, voice, or character type. Sometimes even professional actors make this mistake. ***These mistakes are a big deal because they suggest the performer is not a literate theatre artist.***

Just as bad are the rotating parade of the same 20-30 songs and monologues. There's so much great material out there, yet very few people go in search of something lesser known. While adjudicators try to be objective, it's hard to hear Biff's famous monologue from the end of *Death of a Salesman* again and again without making comparisons to other performances or even reciting it in their head.

This is why choosing well-written, under-performed material is important. It will engage the adjudicators, getting them to pay attention to you and not some well-worn monologue or song they'll hear three other times that day. And the great news is there's so much good repertoire out there in every genre imaginable that's perfect for you. It just takes a bit of research to find it.

In this chapter, we're going to focus on how and where you can find audition repertoire. In our experience, you will probably need 4 different songs and 2-3 monologues depending on various institutions' requirements. Remember: the material you choose says just as much about you as your talent does. Make sure you're putting your best foot forward with smart material.

There are some general things you should remember when picking a song or a monologue:

**Choose something age and gender appropriate**. You shouldn't be singing "I'm Still Here" from *Follies* at age 17. As Elaine Stritch would have said to you, "Where have you been?!"

And it's great that, as a 16 year old girl, you think you can nail the title role of *King Lear*. But even if you can, that doesn't mean you should. He's a 70 year old man. You're not Patrick Stewart. There is plenty of great material out there for performers your age.

Likewise, if you're a cisgender (meaning someone whose gender identity corresponds with the sex they were assigned at birth) male, singing "Maybe This Time" from *Cabaret*, is a no-no. <u>*Loving the song is not enough of a good reason to sing it*</u>. Yes, you should personally connect to the material, but it must still meet the qualifications of being age and gender appropriate. You can sing other songs that don't fall into this category in a cabaret, or other setting... just not in an audition.

If you're a transgender or agender young artist, we recommend you present material that feels most appropriate to you. We recognize you will probably not find many songs or monologues that reflect your personal experience. Know that contemporary cisgender, transgender, and agender dramatists are changing that. In the meantime, seek smart teachers and coaches who will help you find material that allows you to feel most comfortable as a performing artist.

**Ask yourself what you do well**. Again, your teacher or coach will be able to help you here. If you have a strong legit sound, pick material that showcases that. If you've got great comic timing, perform something funny. Chances are you already know what you can and like to do.

**Find material that "feels like you."** If you find songs and monologues you can identify with, it will be that much easier to learn and make your own. Plus adjudicators are trying to get to know you at a college audition. Picking material closely aligned with who you really are is a great way to do that. So make sure

sure at least one of your songs and monologues fits this requirement. We'll talk about this more in the next section.

**Find something you like.** This sounds like a no-brainer, but you're going to be doing this material a <u>lot</u>! Don't pick something just because everyone tells you it is perfect for you if you hate it. It will show.

**Avoid obscene material.** This may also seem obvious, but we've seen it in auditions many times, so… keep away from material with cursing, racial epithets, or overt sexual content. An example of this would be "MUE" ("My Unfortunate Erection") from *The 25th Annual Putnam County Spelling Bee* or monologues from Sarah Kane's *4:48 Psychosis*. Again, it brings more attention to the material than you. There's no reason to potentially offend anyone and there's plenty of good material without it.

Here are some further things to consider, specific to songs and monologues.

<u>Choosing a Song</u>

"Not for the Life of Me" from *Thoroughly Modern Millie*. "Pulled" from *The Addams Family*. "All I Need is the Girl" from *Gypsy*. All three are fantastic songs. All three are relatively age-appropriate. And none of them should be sung at a college audition because they're overdone.

We can't emphasize this enough: performing an overdone song in an audition can be a huge mistake. You are more likely to be compared with others that sing the same songs. That's not what you want in an audition situation.

Many musical theatre programs have created a list of songs to avoid on their websites under information about auditions. Make sure to pay close attention to each program's restrictions. We've also compiled a list of composers, shows, and songs we believe should be on the "no fly zone" in **Appendix C**.

So how do you find songs that aren't inappropriate or overdone?

First, you need to know your voice type. Your voice teacher should be able to tell you this. Here are the most common voice types for a high school student: legit soprano, high belt/mix, legit mezzo, belt mezzo, tenor, and baritone. **Women: you are not both a legit soprano and a mezzo belter. That's not a thing.** You might be able to sing legit and belt, but your voice type is your voice type. Knowing that will have a direct influence on the repertoire you choose.

Then consider your character type. Are you an ingenue? Funny best friend? Character tenor? Leading man? There are lots of different types and the clearer you are on yours, the better. This is where a voice teacher, acting teacher, or audition coach with a strong musical theatre background will be helpful.

You should start looking for actual audition song(s) only after you have this information. When searching for audition material, here are some other things to consider:

**Show legato (flowing) vocal line.** Young performers love to bring in fast, wordy songs, which are either comedic or contemporary. Even if they're well-written, these songs may not showcase your voice in an audition. It's like wearing a really "loud" sweater: people will pay more attention to the sweater than you. Singing a Golden Age musical theatre (1940's - 1960's, depending on who you ask) ballad or uptempo is going to be a better option. This will allow the adjudicators to actually hear your voice and it will ground your work as a singing actor.

Golden Age… It doesn't seem as fun as singing something contemporary. We get it. We love contemporary songs too. But that doesn't mean you can't have a healthy diet of Golden Age *and* contemporary musical theatre songs in your book. To us, that's the smarter solution.

**Think of the pianist.** Giving your audition pianist a difficult song will make them less available to be a good collaborator. If the pianist doesn't know the piece, they will most likely play loudly (we tend to play louder when sight reading). And the pianist will probably resent you if the accompaniment is obnoxiously hard. All of this will increase the chances of your audition not going well.

Many people say, "Don't ever sing Sondheim or Jason Robert Brown at an audition." That seems a little drastic to us - it depends on the song. There's a big difference between Sondheim's "I Remember" or "Take Me to the World" from *Evening Primrose* and "Everybody Says Don't" from *Anyone Can Whistle*. The songs from *Evening Primrose* are easy to sight-read. "Everybody Says Don't" is not. Similarly, there's a difference between singing Jason Robert Brown's "Christmas Lullaby" (which is sight readable) and "She Cries" (which is not) from *Songs for a New World*.

**Choose at least one song you can sing sick**. It's very tempting to choose audition material that's flashy and demanding. But what if you get sick? It might be smart to choose one song that isn't as rangey in the event you're vocally compromised. Do you take medications? Make sure you know how they affect you when you sing and choose repertoire that will give you the appropriate flexibility.

**Consider the possible song order as you choose your material.** If you have the option of singing two songs, you should always lead with a song that shows your legit voice and legato (connected) vocal line (legit songs allows adjudicators can hear your voice better than some contemporary or pop/rock songs, depending on how they're written). You can then follow that with something contrasting. Often times that might mean you'll start with your Golden Age piece then move to a contemporary piece. Keep this in mind when choosing material, as it may impact what you settle on.

What about *where* to look for good songs?

Start with your voice teacher or audition coach. They should know several appropriate songs that will meet all your audition requirements. Consider using a lesson or two to simply sing through a several different audition songs to see what you enjoy singing and what fits in your voice. Give each song you sing through a real chance. Sometimes you might not like it right away. Keep your options open and see what songs seem to bubble up to the top of your brain when you think about what you'd like to perform at your auditions.

Don't solely rely on your teachers for support, though. Do your own research. If you're an avid musical theatre fan, we're sure you're aware of current running shows and others you've either seen or performed in yourself. Go online and Google things like "college audition songs," or "great audition songs." You'll need to listen to a lot of repertoire and cross-reference it with your programs' requirements.

When you're ready, go to websites like halleonard.com or sheetmusicdirect.com to purchase the sheet music. Sometimes you'll be able to buy the individual song and sometimes you'll have to buy a selection book or anthology. Either way, both of these sites will have reliable scores for purchase.

**You should always sing your musical theatre songs in the original show or selection book key.** By altering the key, you can potentially the change feeling of the song, which influences the character's journey. It also causes the audition pianist distress when they're used to playing a song in one key and are presented with a completely different key.

Where else can you look? Dare we suggest the library? Some libraries have a surprisingly good collection of musical scores. If you live in or close to New York City, visit the New York Performing Arts Library at Lincoln Center. They have a breathtaking assortment of full scores, selection books, and anthologies. If you don't live in a major metropolitan area, visit one, or check out the library at one of the colleges you're looking at. How cool would it be to find your song at the place you plan to sing it?! Also consider interlibrary loan - sometimes you can actually order scores from other libraries in completely different states.

If you're looking for contemporary songs, visit us at ContemporaryMusicalTheatre.com. We have hundreds of appropriate audition songs available, searchable by voice and song type. We offer annual, monthly and "quick pass" 3-day subscriptions - perfect for your (or your parents') wallet.

How about where *not* to buy your music? We have thoughts on that too.

**Do not buy musical theatre songs on musicnotes.com!** They do a lot of things well, but many of the musical theatre songs (especially Golden Age) are not in the right key, are weirdly arranged, or have wrong notes and rhythms. **Exception:** If you're preparing a pop/rock song for a college audition, it's completely appropriate to buy it on musicnotes.com and change the key to fit your voice.

While we like the site and its owners, we find the repertoire on newmusicaltheatre.com to be very popular and, therefore, overdone in auditions.

Finally, avoid the Hal Leonard Musical Theatre Anthology collection. Rick Walters has done a fantastic job of putting together this extensive assortment of musical theatre songs, but sadly it's the first stop for most teachers and students, which makes most of these songs overdone.

We've talked a lot about what not to sing (see **Appendix C**). What about some recommendations of great songs not many performers know about? See **Appendix D** for some of our favorite underperformed song recommendations by voice type.

Choosing a Monologue

Choosing material is one of the most challenging parts of the audition process. Finding two or three monologues to represent you is no easy task. They need to be age, gender, and ethnically appropriate. They should also be of contrasting content styles: one comedic, one dramatic, one classical. Different schools will have different requirements, but if you prepare three one-minute monologues in these three contrasting styles, you should not have to prepare anything else, especially for any one particular audition.

Just as you will when choosing your songs, you must figure out your type. During her time at NYU Steinhardt, Laura studied with "audition doctor," Fred Silver, who wrote the (still relevant) book *Auditioning for the Musical Theatre: One of the Country's Leading Musical Audition Coaches Prepares You to Get the Parts You Want* (Penguin Books). On the first day of class, Mr. Silver asked each student to go out to the hall, then re-enter and "audition." One at a time, students came in, crossed the room and gave their music to the pianist. But as soon as one them walked in front of the class and got ready to begin their actual audition, Mr. Silver would put his hand up and say, "Stop!" Then he would ask the class a series of questions: "What do you think she is going to sing?" "Is it going to be comedic or dramatic?" "How old does she look?" "Does her outfit match the kind of material she looks right for?" Then he would say, "That is what the people behind the table just did as you were crossing the room and talking to the pianist. Your job as a performer is to help complete the picture those people just painted, not confuse it."

So what is your type? Start with an honest self-assessment: Do you look your age? or do you look older or younger? What is your physical type? Skinny or heavyset? Nerdy or smoldering? What is your voice type? Do you have a high squeaky voice? or is your voice low and dramatic? What kind of vibe do you give off? Fun and flirty? Quiet and standoffish?

If you're not sure what your type is, ask (trusted) teachers and friends. This can be quite helpful even if you think you know your type, since others don't view us the way we view ourselves.

After you've considered your type, here are some additional things to look out for:

**Make sure the monologue you choose is from a play.** You should not pick a monologue from a screenplay or perform an "original" (or stand-alone) monologue. Pay attention to this as some schools have specific rules about the source of audition material.

**Don't pick something identifiable with a certain performer or that you've heard lots of other people performing.** Your goal is to choose material that will help you stand out. You don't want to be compared to someone else.

**Consider monologue order as you choose your material.** When you have two contrasting pieces, plan to start with the one you feel most comfortable with. There's always the possibility that you may be cut off after your first selection, so put your best foot forward.

With that said, how do you go about finding appropriate monologues?

Start with what _not_ to do. Many colleges actually provide lists of monologues they do not want you to perform on their websites, so check there first. Visit **Appendix E** for our list of overdone monologues. Remember, you want to stand out, not to be compared to 27 other people who performed your same monologue that day.

Monologue books can sometimes be a good place to start. As opposed to musical anthologies, there are lots of options and there are multiple monologue collections created specifically for young performers. If you're lucky enough to live in New York City, visit the Drama Bookshop (250 West 40th Street, New York, NY 10018), where they not only have a large selection to choose from but also have very helpful and knowledgeable staff (if you're outside of NYC, visit their online store at dramabookshop.com). Laura spent multiple hours there researching monologues for this book. Her technique? Pull a play off the shelf, look at the character list, and see if any characters are 18 or under, then start reading. It was time consuming, but it worked.

New play anthologies are another place to find exciting and underperformed plays that haven't yet made it into monologue books. Visit the websites: playscripts.com, samuelfrench.com, and dramatists.com. Search by audience "teen" or browse anthologies to find age appropriate characters.

Another route is to look up regional theatres known for doing new and interesting plays. You can also follow actors who are your type on social media. See what plays they're performing in and look to see if they have monologues you could use.

If this seems too overwhelming, you can hire an audition coach, who will have their own library of material. But make sure they are familiar with the college audition requirements. If they hand you one or two of the monologues on our overdone list - move on. You can always Skype with a coach if there are none near where you live.

Next, read the monologue out loud. Reading in your head uses completely different parts of your brain. Make sure it feels comfortable coming out of your mouth. It may sound silly, but sometimes that monologue you liked on the page has a very different feeling once you're saying it out loud.

Once you find one monologue you like, aim to find a contrasting monologue for your second piece. When we say contrasting, we don't just mean in terms of the genre (comedic, dramatic, classic) but also in the range of what it highlights about you. No one-minute monologue is going to be able to showcase all your talents or traits, so what you don't show off in one monologue, try to show off in another. If your dramatic monologue character is shy and introspective, find a comedic monologue where the character is quirky and bold.

Once you have several monologues you like, read each of the plays they come from. We cannot stress how important this is. A monologue is out of context. There is much more to be gained by knowing how it fits into the larger construct, including character and situational information you will not get from a monologue book. This may influence whether or not the monologue is a good audition choice for you and help realistically portray it if it is.

Many college auditors will be familiar with the source material of the monologue you've chosen and you don't want to be caught unaware if they ask you about it.

See **Appendix F** for a list of recommended monologues by type.

## STUDENT

Everything you need to know is above. And it's *a lot*, isn't it? Now you see why it's so important you start looking for material the summer between your junior and senior year. It's going to take a while to find things that meet all the requirements and inspire you to perform your best. Take your time, use the resources in this book, and those at your disposal. Work with an audition coach if you can. All these things will help ensure you stand out come audition season.

## TEACHER

You play such an important role in helping the young artist choose smart repertoire for their college auditions. Most of what we've seen is well-worn and will not help your student be heard as a unique individual.

Students often don't know who they are at their age. It probably won't surprise you that even college seniors struggle with this as they're putting together their professional audition books. Encourage the student to try lots of different material to see where they naturally gravitate. This might further illuminate where they can look for good material. It's very important to emphasize the difference between what they love and what they should perform. This shouldn't have to mean they sacrifice being excited about their audition material. There's enough great material out there to meet anyone's specific needs.

It's important that you stay current and constantly refresh your library of material. Because we're both active freelance teachers, we are always on the look-out for new (to us), under-performed material. If you have friends or colleagues who are adjudicators, as them what they do and don't want to hear. This is an ever-changing list and it's important you keep your finger on the pulse of what's happening year to year. This investment of time will reap great benefits to the students and your growing studio.

Please look at **Appendices C-F** for helpful information on overdone and recommended audition material.

## PARENT

Unless you're a musical theatre professional, there's probably not much you can do to help here. What you can do is keep referring your young artist to the chart you created together (see **Appendix A**) and frequently review the audition requirements. Every college asks for something a little different, so you can help your child make sure the repertoire they've chosen meets all of the necessary criteria. That will be a big help to them.

Review important deadlines and anything that may have fallen off the radar where paperwork is concerned. If your child is auditioning at upwards of 15 schools, you'll be spinning a lot of plates! Even the most organized child will miss something. Consider setting an hour aside a week to review where your child is with each college. "Team meetings" can be a helpful way to make sure everyone is on the same page and getting things done when they need to be.

Also, expect to open up your wallet a bit while they purchase plays and scores. Musical selection books and anthologies are more expensive ($16-$25), and aren't always the best bargain for the young artist, because not everything in them is age (or gender) appropriate. Purchasing single pieces is generally the most cost-effective way to go. Individual songs usually range from $6-$10.

For monologues, purchasing anthologies *is* the more cost effective way to go. Monologue books will range from $12-$20, but since there are whole anthologies dedicated to young performers, they will get about 50 monologues in one book. After your child chooses their monologues, they should buy the plays they are from so they understand the context of the monologue. Plays can range from $10-$15 but, depending on their selection, it's possible they can borrow them from a good library. Some are also available online for free if the play is in public domain.

This can be a stressful time for your child. The reality of the challenges of this degree and career will hopefully be setting in around this time. We know you'll be supportive but not cloying as they navigate their way through the maze of repertoire to come up with songs and monologues that illuminate who they are.

# CHAPTER 5: HOW DO I CUT MY MATERIAL FOR AUDITIONS?

Why only 16- or 32-bars? Why only 1 or 2 minutes for a monologue? What could adjudicators possibly see in such a short amount of time?

It only takes 45-60 seconds for an astute educator to focus in on several things: the performer's technical skills, expressiveness, and ability to adapt. Many times they can simultaneously hear or see if a young artist's technical work isn't serving them and discern whether or not those issues are easily fixed. They usually can decipher if nerves are getting in the way. And based on their background and knowledge of the institution, they can accurately ascertain whether or not a student is right for their program.

Yes, all that in 60 seconds.

The adjudicator also takes in everything you do in the room, from how you talk to the pianist, how you slate and, of course, your choice of material. All these things are the framework you create before you begin presenting your audition material.

In this chapter, we'll discuss how to choose audition cuts that will meet your various audition requirements and set you up for success in the audition room. Picking an audition cut is just as important as choosing the right song. There's something truly cringe worthy about a poorly selected audition cut.

Imagine us singing this to you:

Happy Birthday to you!
Happy Birthday to you!
Happy Birthday, dear reader.....

That's a horrible place to end. Many young performers, however, deliver these kinds of "cliffhanger cuts," as we call them.

Alternatively, imagine performing a monologue and getting cut off with a "thank you" or "time" right before the ending. That would stink.

Also, think about the adjudicators. We've both been held hostage by an auditioning performer because their cuts were too long. We either felt guilty or angry for having to cut them off. When the performer doesn't respect the audition requirements, it doesn't inspire our confidence in their abilities. You don't want to put the adjudicators in that position, especially during a long audition day.

The above examples underscore a common problem in many high school students' audition cuts. Poorly chosen audition cuts can make you seem just as inexperienced as a bad audition song or monologue.

Choosing Song Cuts

Most colleges will request 16-bar cuts of the required audition songs. What does that actually mean? It means you should prepare either a 16-bar ballad or 32-bar up-tempo. Both should be acceptable in an audition situation that asks for 16-bar cuts. Normally, up-tempos are in a fast 4/4 or 2/2 (cut time). If you don't know if a song is an up-tempo, ask a vocal coach or accompanist for help.

Let's start by asking one basic question: what do you want the audition cut to show? There are three answers:

- **Range.** This doesn't mean you have to show the very highest and lowest note you can sing, but the cut should clearly indicate your voice type.
- **A character's journey from point A to Z.** The cut must show a character discovering or expressing something that's new to them, with a clear obstacle and high stakes.
- **Prove you're a smart performer.** The cut must convey you understand musical theatre song structure.

Given that you're probably going to sing something Golden Age, at least to start (hint, hint...), this makes your life fairly simple. Most Golden Age musical theatre songs are usually written in a very specific way, which makes them easier to cut. They tend to have a verse, followed by a 32-bar refrain. Sometimes there's a coda on the end, sometimes not.

Is all of this Greek to you? Let's break down some of the terminology.

Golden Age songs tend to be in verse-chorus format. This mean there's a verse that sets up the story of the song and a refrain (or chorus) that is the actual meat of the song. *You should never sing the verse of a song as part of your audition cut.* Only choose material from the refrain. And think of a coda as a musical tag at the end of a song.

The other things Golden Age songs tend to have in common are their structure, which is often AABA. No, that's not a misspelling of the 70's rock band ABBA (whose music was the basis of the jukebox musical *Mamma Mia!*). AABA is a very common song form in musical theatre because it allows the character to have a discovery in the song, moving the plot and character's development forward. As you would probably assume, the A Sections all have the same (or almost identical) melody and rhyme scheme. The B Section opens up the song, offering new (dramatic and musical) ideas that deepen the character's journey.

While there are many other common song forms, we're going to focus on AABA for now. Let's look at "So in Love" from *Kiss Me, Kate* by Cole Porter. We recommend you listen to the song while reading along.

**A SECTION**
Strange dear, but true dear,
When I'm close to you, dear,
The stars fill the sky,
So in love with you am I.

**A SECTION**
Even without you,
My arms fold about you,
You know darling why,
So in love with you am I.

**B SECTION**
In love with the night mysterious,
The night when you first were there,
In love with my joy delirious,
When I knew that you could care,

**A SECTION**
So taunt me, and hurt me,
Deceive me, desert me,
I'm yours, till I die,
So in love,
So in love,
So in love with you, my love, am I.

*"So in Love"*
*from Kiss Me, Kate*
*by Cole Porter*
*reprinted by permission*

Notice the distilled dramatic idea in each stanza:

**A** - I love you.
**A** - I love you even when you're gone.
**B** - This isn't a passing fancy. I've known this for a while.
**A** - There's nothing you can do to change how I feel.

With these types of songs, you can usually do two things: sing the B Section to the end or sing the first and last A Sections. Either will give you the arc of the character's journey. Taking "So in Love" as our example, here's the B and final A.

**B SECTION**
In love with the night mysterious,
The night when you first were there,
In love with my joy delirious,
When I knew that you could care,

**A SECTION**
So taunt me, and hurt me,
Deceive me, desert me,
I'm yours, till I die.
So in love,
So in love,
So in love with you, my love, am I.

Or, you can sing the first and last A sections which, in this case, feels like a more complete thought:

**1st A SECTION**
Strange dear, but true dear,
When I'm close to you, dear,
The stars fill the sky,
So in love with you am I.

**Final A SECTION**
So taunt me, and hurt me,
Deceive me, desert me,
I'm yours, till I die,
So in love,
So in love,
So in love with you, my love, am I.

Again, this shows a journey in thought and works very well musically.

If you decide to sing the first and last A Sections, it will take a little cutting and pasting. You need to clearly mark you music so the audition pianist can play their best for you. You can do this by neatly crossing out the sections you're not going to sing or (even better) cutting and pasting it onto a separate piece of blank paper. If you have an adept vocal coach, they may be able to create for you a clean 16- or 32-bar cut in Finale or Sibelius (music engraving software). Either way, you need to make sure the cut is clearly marked and easy to read. Look at **Appendix I** for some examples of auditions cuts.

What if there's a coda at the end of your chosen song (as there is with "So in Love"), making the cut more than a 16-bar ballad or 32-bar up-tempo? The rule of thumb is: finish the thought. No one is counting measures during your audition. Of course, if a song goes on much longer than it should, you will most likely be stopped. Use discretion. If the cut is 20 bars long for a 16-bar cut or 36 bars long for a 32-bar cut, that's still acceptable.

What if there's a key change in the middle of the song? Key changes can be fine, as long as they fall at the beginning or the middle of the cut and are clearly marked (it's best to highlight changes in the key and time signature for the pianist to draw their attention to them). Many young artists who start their cut at the key change will ask the audition pianist for an introduction in the old key, which makes finding their first note in the new key very challenging. Work with your voice teacher or vocal coach to create a lead-in to the audition cut that works for you, or simply ask for a "bell tone" (your starting pitch).

Contemporary songs don't always cut as easily because they sometimes use different song structures (i.e. story songs, pop/rock song forms, etc..). In general, you should try to cut 16 or 32 bars from the end. Sometimes there's a good case to be made for choosing a cut from the middle of a song. That's fine, as long as it makes for a complete thought. Again, see **Appendix I** for examples of audition cuts.

Regardless of the genre of musical theatre song, make sure you run your audition cut by your voice teacher, vocal coach, or musical director. They should be able to tell you whether or not it works. It can be disheartening to find a song you like but realize it doesn't cut well for an audition. This is why you always want to have other options.

On the off-chance the folks behind the table ask for a different cut of your song, have two copies of your chosen audition song(s) in your book: one full copy without markings and another with your 32- and/or 16-bar cut. Of course, this means you must know the entire song. We'll talk more about that later.

It's quite possible you'll create two different cuts of the same song depending on audition requirements. Many students have both 32- and 16-bar cuts of their songs so they can adapt to any situation on the day of the audition. That's a smart move.

Choosing Monologue Cuts

Most monologues you choose are not going to be one minute long, so you will probably need to edit them to meet the time requirements. We recommend you cut all your monologues to one minute because then they will be appropriate for the majority or your auditions. Even if some schools request "one- to two-minute monologues," they'll be happy to have you perform just for one minute. This will still give them plenty of time to see what they need to and might also encourage them to ask for another monologue.

Sometimes you will get lucky, and find a monologue that you don't need to cut or edit. More often, to tell a complete story you will need to do some editing, sometimes including a few lines of dialogue from before or after the monologue.

Let's look at a monologue from *The Rivals* by Richard Brinsley Sheridan:

LYDIA
Then before we are interrupted, let me impart to you some of my distress! I know your gentle nature will sympathize with me, though your prudence may condemn me! My letters have informed you of my whole connection with Beverley; but I have lost him, Julia! My aunt has discovered our intercourse by a note she intercepted, and has confined me ever since! Yet, would you believe it? she has absolutely fallen in love with a tall Irish baronet she

65

met one night since we have been here, at Lady Macshuffle's rout.

JULIA

You jest, Lydia!

LYDIA

No, upon my word. She really carries on a kind of correspondence with him, under a feigned name though, till she chooses to be known to him: but it is a Delia or a Celia, I assure you.

JULIA

Then, surely, she is now more indulgent to her niece.

LYDIA

Quite the contrary. Since she has discovered her own frailty, she is become more suspicious of mine. Then I must inform you of another plague! That odious Acres is to be in Bath to-day; so that I protest I shall be teased out of all spirits!

JULIA

Come, come, Lydia, hope for the best—Sir Anthony shall use his interest with Mrs. Malaprop.

LYDIA

But you have not heard the worst. Unfortunately, I had quarreled with my poor Beverley, just before my aunt made the discovery, and I have not seen him since, to make it up.

JULIA

What was his offence?

LYDIA

Nothing at all! But, I don't know how it was, as often as we had been together, we had never had a quarrel, and, somehow, I was afraid he would never give me an opportunity. So, last Thursday, I wrote a letter to myself, to inform myself that Beverley was at that time paying his addresses to another woman. I signed it *your friend unknown*, showed it to Beverley, charged him with his falsehood, put myself in a violent passion, and vowed I'd never see him more.

JULIA

And you let him depart so, and have not seen him since?

LYDIA

'Twas the next day my aunt found the matter out. I intended only to have teased him three days and a half, and now I've lost him forever.

*The Rivals*
*by Richard Brinsley Sheridan*
*Public Domain*

You'll notice that after Lydia's short monologue I have included part of a scene with dialogue for two actors. To enable Lydia to tell more of a complete story, you will first need to cut out Julia's lines and string Lydia's lines together like this:

LYDIA

Then before we are interrupted, let me impart to you some of my distress! I know your gentle nature will sympathize with me, though your prudence may condemn me! My letters have informed you of my whole connection with Beverley; but I have lost him, Julia! My aunt has discovered our intercourse by a note she intercepted, and has confined me ever since! Yet, would you believe it? she has absolutely fallen in love with a tall Irish baronet she met one night since we have been here, at Lady Macshuffle's rout. No, upon my word. She really carries on a kind of correspondence with him, under a feigned name though, till she chooses to be known to him: but it is a Delia or a Celia, I assure you. Quite the contrary. Since she has discovered her own frailty, she is become more suspicious of mine. Then I must inform you of another plague! That odious Acres is to be in Bath to-day; so that I protest I shall be teased out of all spirits! But you have not heard the worst. Unfortunately, I had quarreled with my poor Beverley, just before my aunt made the discovery, and I have not seen him since, to make it up. Nothing at all! But, I don't know how it was, as often as we had been together, we had never had a quarrel, and, somehow, I was afraid he would never give me an opportunity. So, last Thursday, I wrote a letter to myself, to inform myself that Beverley was at that time paying his addresses to another woman. I signed it *your friend unknown*, showed it to Beverley, charged him with his falsehood, put myself in a violent passion, and vowed I'd never see him more. 'Twas the next day my aunt found the matter out. I intended only to have teased him three days and a half, and now I've lost him forever.

Now we hear Lydia's full story.

Before cutting the monologue, read it out loud, timing yourself. Be sure not to rush through it. You want to leave time for the acting beats (more on this in the next chapter). *The Rivals* monologue is about two minutes long so one minute of material will need to be cut.

When beginning to make cuts, you need to make sure the monologue maintains a strong beginning, middle and end. This doesn't mean you have to keep the very beginning or end of the piece, but you do need to be sure you're still telling a complete story.

Once you've read *The Rivals*, you will know this monologue happens very early in the play and that Lydia has just been reunited with her cousin, Julia. They haven't seen each other in a while so Lydia needs to tell her everything that has happened since their last meeting.

Here is one possible cut of this monologue:

### LYDIA

Then before we are interrupted, let me impart to you some of my distress! I know your gentle nature will sympathize with me, though your prudence may condemn me! My letters have informed you of my whole connection with Beverley; but I have lost him, Julia! My aunt has discovered our intercourse by a note she intercepted, and has confined me ever since! ~~Yet, would you believe it? she has absolutely fallen in love with a tall Irish baronet she met one night since we have been here, at Lady Macshuffle's rout. No, upon my word. She really carries on a kind of correspondence with him, under a feigned name though, till she chooses to be known to him: but it is a Delia or a Celia, I assure you. Quite the contrary. Since she has discovered her own frailty, she is become more suspicious of mine. Then I must inform you of another plague! That odious Acres is to be in Bath to-day; so that I protest I shall be teased out of all spirits!~~ But you have not heard the worst. Unfortunately, I had quarreled with my poor Beverley, just before my aunt made the discovery, and I have not seen him since, to make it up. Nothing at all! But, I don't know how it was, as often as we had been together, we had never had a quarrel, and, somehow, I was afraid he would never give me an opportunity. So, last Thursday, I wrote a letter to myself, to inform myself that Beverley was at that time paying his addresses to another woman. I signed it *your friend unknown*, showed it to Beverley, charged him with his falsehood, put myself in a violent passion, and vowed I'd never see him more. 'Twas the next day my aunt found the matter out. I intended only to have teased him three days and a half, and now I've lost him forever.

The focus of Lydia's story is what happens between her and her suitor, Beverley. If we just focus on that plot, we can cut out the information about her aunt. Now the monologue tells a complete story for Lydia, and her character arc feels complete.

Can you edit out any parts of the monologue you'd like or change the words? That's where it starts to get a bit dicey. You have to be careful not to alter the playwright's original intent with your edits. If the monologue becomes too hard to cut, you should look elsewhere. This is where an acting teacher or audition coach will be very helpful.

Finding the right audition cuts can be as time consuming as finding the audition material itself. Don't assume the first thing you try is your best option. Try several different versions of your song and monologue cuts and see what makes the most sense to you and your teachers.

## STUDENT

Broken record alert: you must be clear about any audition requirements and make sure anyone who is helping you find and cut material is on the same page. While you may have help, at the end of the day, you're the one who's going to be in the audition room. You want to make intelligent decisions that create a favorable impression.

Don't rely on anthologies that do this work for you. Yes, there are some books that have audition cuts all picked out for you. As you would probably suspect, those will be overdone. Do this hard work yourself because it will shine through when you present your work.

## TEACHER

Sometimes students don't have the dramaturgical skills to make smart cuts in their audition material. Use this as an opportunity to talk to them about the structure of the material and why it works as it is. Help them talk through the beats of the song or monologue so they can see what (if anything) might be extraneous in an audition situation. This will help them better understand the craft of writing and positively inform their learning process.

It's most important that each audition cut have a beginning, middle and end. As you saw from the examples we gave above, it's fairly simple to shape material in a way that meets the requirements while also completing a thought. And yet, so many students bring in material that doesn't do this. It puts them at a disadvantage in the audition room. Therefore, your input is incredibly important.

Having said that, we encourage you to let the student take the lead on this, guiding them as necessary. If they intend on pursuing theatre as a career, this is a skill they will need to hone for the rest of their life. Best to start now!

# PARENT

Unless you're a musical theatre professional, you'll most likely sit this one out. The best advice we can give is to make sure your young artist has access to a smart teacher(s) and/or coach(es), who will help them figure out the best audition cut(s) for their auditions. If this is a financial impossibility, reach out to your child's high school drama teacher or other professionals you might know (director, actor, etc....). It's not impossible for the student to do some of this work on their own. Hopefully this chapter will be a helpful guide. With some hard work, you and your child can figure this out together. Listen to the material together and make sure they're telling a complete and satisfying story.

It would be easy to think that the hard work is over once the audition material is picked. Unfortunately, this is not true. In fact, we believe how well you do in the audition room is almost always a direct result of how you practiced. We have very specific thoughts on how you can prepare for success in and out of the practice room.

## Learning Audition Material

You're going to be learning a lot of new material in the next several months. You need a clear game plan on how to juggle the technical demands that come with this. It all has to do with taking it apart.

### *Preparing Monologues*

After you choose and cut your monologue, the first thing you should do is read the entire play from which it's taken. We cannot emphasize enough how important this is. You need to know who your character is talking to and what happened in the moments before the monologue begins. As you read the play, make notes about your character. These could be things your character says and does but it could also be how other characters react to your character. Sometimes the playwright will write a character description at the beginning of the script. Sometimes there will be clues in the stage directions. Sometimes it will just be your reaction to your character's actions. Note everything. No detail is too small.

Next, figure out what the action of the character is during the monologue. By that we mean what are they *doing*. This is also sometime called "motivation" or "I want." First, try to choose a single "action verb" to play for the whole monologue. An action verb has a physical or mental action you can act. You can look up lists of action verbs online but some examples would be "to fight" "to solve" "to demand." Not all verbs are action verbs. "To like," "to think," and "to feel" are examples of non-action verbs. If there is no action, it is not an action verb. For example, instead of "to like," you might choose "to flirt" or "to seduce." Those are actions you can play as an actor. The stronger the action verb, the easier it will be for you to work with.

Let's go back to our monologue from *The Rivals* (Chapter 5) and choose one action verb that could be applied to the whole thing. You could pick "to plead" if you think Lydia is trying to get Julia to help her. But you also could choose "to enchant" or "to manipulate." There's not a right and wrong choice and different actors will choose different actions when they play the same role. But do you see how differently you would perform the monologue with these different choices?

This sounds tedious and overwhelming. When you are first starting this process you will probably find it very challenging. Don't give up. Even professional actors struggle with this process and may go through several different choices of actions until they find the one that seems to fit best. But figuring out *why* a character acts is critical to creating a believable character.

Once you've chosen your main action, the next step is to break down the monologue into individual beats. A single monologue will have many different ideas and actions. Each time the action changes it is called a "beat." Go through the monologue and mark each new thought with a slash ("/"). Let's look at one way *The Rivals* monologue could be divided into beats:

LYDIA
Then before we are interrupted, let me impart to you some of my distress! I know your gentle nature will sympathize with me, though your prudence may condemn me! / My letters have informed you of my whole connection with Beverley; but I have lost him, Julia! My aunt has discovered our intercourse by a note she intercepted, and has confined me ever since! / But you have not heard the worst. Unfortunately, I had quarreled with my poor Beverley, just before my aunt made the discovery, and I have not seen him since, to make it up. Nothing at all! / But, I don't know how it was, as often as we had been

74

together, we had never had a quarrel, and, somehow, I was afraid he would never give me an opportunity. / So, last Thursday, I wrote a letter to myself, to inform myself that Beverley was at that time paying his addresses to another woman. I signed it *your friend unknown*, showed it to Beverley, charged him with his falsehood, put myself in a violent passion, and vowed I'd never see him more. / 'Twas the next day my aunt found the matter out. / I intended only to have teased him three days and a half, and now I've lost him forever.

Next you will want to attach an "action verb" to each individual beat. Let's say you chose the action verb "to plead" for the whole monologue. Now you need to choose multiple verbs for each beat that can all be used "to plead." For the first beat, she could "confide." For the second, she could "entice." For the third, she could "dramatize." All of these verbs are ways Lydia could plead her case to Julia.

There is not one "right" way to break down the beats in a monologue. A lot depends on how you think the character develops their own thoughts. But that's why the process is important. To create a believable character, you need to know how and why your character moves from one idea to the next. The process is time consuming but once you put in the work, you will be able to create a much more believable character.

Next, you need to figure out your "moment before." What happened right before the monologue begins? Where are you? Who is with you in the scene? What did another character say or do to your character to launch you into the monologue? Here is one way reading the play becomes critically important. Knowing these details will help you create a believable situation. Many actors launch into a monologue without any clear sense of the moment before. The moment before should have an action verb as well and that beat should happen before you open your mouth to speak.

Once you know where you are, who you're talking to, and what you want, it's time to learn your monologue. Notice we said "learn," and not memorize. There is a difference between just knowing the words and actually *understanding* them. The technique we use with our students will help you learn your monologue faster and connect to the language and content quicker. To begin, read the monologue out loud. Don't work too hard to act - just try to read and listen to the story you are telling. Next, put the paper face down and say as much of the monologue as you remember. This may sound scary, but you'll be amazed by how much you remember. Then, pick up the paper and read the monologue out loud again, identifying what you remembered and what you forgot. Often times, what you forgot can be as telling as what you remembered: unusual language, foreign or repeated words. Make a note of them and then repeat the process until you have "learned" the whole monologue. Using this method, you will learn material faster and better understand what you're saying. *Note*: Be sure you eventually learn all the words in your monologue. Don't paraphrase at your audition!

Another great way to learn your monologue is writing it out by hand. A 2011 study led by Associate Professor Anne Mangen at the University of Stavanger (Norway) explained that, when writing by hand, the brain receives feedback from our motor actions. This helps to strengthen the learning process. Plus, you will quickly see where you are paraphrasing. Another benefit of this learning tool is that you can do it silently when it's inappropriate to say the monologue out loud: like on the school bus, or when you're at the library.

As you learn your monologue, make sure to continue working through the character's actions and objectives. Very often, we see young actors make the mistake of simply reciting the text of the monologue. That's not acting, even if it's honest. Acting is activating the character's given circumstances and fighting for what they want. Make sure you know how and why your character transitions from one beat to the next.

Lastly, be sure to practice a strong start and finish to your monologue. Take time (5-10 seconds) before you begin. Many students make the mistake of launching into their monologue without taking adequate time beforehand. This is a wasted

76

opportunity. Never let your nerves stop you from taking time to prepare. Taking 10 seconds before you begin speaking to prepare can be the difference between success or failure.

Close your eyes, take a deep breath, imagine your "moment before," then open your eyes. Focus on a spot eye level (not right at any one person) and "see" the character you are speaking to. Know what your character wants. THEN begin your monologue. At the end of your monologue, make sure your last line feels final. Then gently drop your head and, after a moment, look straight at the adjudicators and say, "thank you."

For a quick outline of the above, see **Appendix G.**

## *Preparing Songs*

Practicing as a singer is really about taking things apart so you understand how the mechanics of your voice and the structure of the song work.

So many students crash and burn when trying to learn the melody, rhythm, and words at the same time. It's almost impossible not to make a mistake. This is because music and language reside on the two different hemispheres of our brain. For this reason, you must completely take the song apart.

This process is very similar to practicing a monologue. First, write out the lyrics of your song as a monologue (not as lyrics or poetry). Why? In musical theatre, it's common for the book writer (who writes the spoken words of a musical) to write a scene, much of which is consumed by the composer and lyricist, who look for the point of most dramatic conflict and put a song in its place. This often means the book writer's text becomes the lyrics or lyrical ideas of the songs. Also, you need to develop your own relationship with the lyric separate from the music because it will inform your acting choices later on.

Once you have learned the lyrics as a monologue (using the system outlined above), you may now begin to learn the song. First intone the lyrics in rhythm. Intoning is like singing, but without musical pitch. It might sound like you're tone deaf, but will engage your support and placement in a very healthy way. Think of it like performing Shakespeare in an amphitheater. You need to make sure your voice carries by being on the breath and finding the resonance. Note that intoning gets you to learn the rhythm and lyrics without the melody.

Next, learn the melody by using three different exercises. Start by singing on a lip or tongue trill to connect the breath to the tone. Follow this with singing the melody on "ni" (knee) to get the bring the tone forward. Finally, if you're able, sing on n + the vowel of the word. For example:

Some    enchanted  evening
nuh    neh-naeh-neh ni-nih.

While this is challenging, you'll find it gets the vowels on the tip of your tongue, bringing clarity to the tone. Note here that you are learning the notes and rhythm without the lyrics.

Now you're ready to mix and match: rotate intoning, lip trills, ni, and n + vowel, switching every time you breathe. Then try a different order.

Only after you've done this should you put the melody, rhythm, and lyrics together.

Once you've learned the song, you'll want to think about the acting beats, much in the same way you did the monologue. Speak the song as a monologue again and see where your interpretation of the lyric either coincides or conflicts with the music. For example, does it feel more natural for you to speak the lyric at a slower tempo than it's sung in the music? Do you find the rhythmic setting of the text different from your normal speech patterns? If so, ask yourself why these differences exist. It may illuminate something important about how the composer set the lyric.

If you're feeling brave, translate the text *while singing* to find your own way of saying the lyric (much in the way we talked about paraphrasing above). See how this influences where you breathe, your dynamics, and the way you shape the phrases.

Your voice teacher should be able to help you with these kinds of details, and they will probably have their own opinions about how to learn a song. Use all this information to get a clear sense of your voice in the song. It will help you sing it with consistency and originality.

Doing the above is actually just the start, though. Now you must more fully research and incorporate the stylistic markers (i.e. how the phrases are shaped specific to the song's genre). For instance, Golden Age songs tend to be sung in a more forthright way while contemporary songs sometimes require delayed or no vibrato. Understanding how to incorporate stylistic markers into your technique will show adjudicators you know something about the song's place in the musical theatre canon, which will set you apart from other auditioning students.

Many young performers make Golden Age songs sound more contemporary. Work with your voice teacher or vocal coach to make sure you're properly presenting each of your songs in the correct style with a healthy technique.

A word about belting here. For most young singers, belt translates to loud and vocally constricted. We have seen only a handful of young singers who have enough technical nuance to navigate belt in a healthy way. It makes sense. It's hard! That's why many teachers don't teach students how to belt until their voices are properly aligned. If you're choosing to belt for an audition because you think it's impressive, choose something else. If you're sure you know how to properly belt with the help of an experienced teacher, great.

Again, keep in mind that, while you will most likely only present 32 or 16 bars of your audition song(s), you should learn and memorize the *entire* song on the off-chance the adjudicators ask to hear a different cut than the one you've presented. This happens in auditions from time to time and you don't want to be caught off guard.

**Do not listen to recordings of the song while you're learning it.** Several years ago, David was working with a young tenor whom he had assigned "I'm Alive" from *Next to Normal* (before it became an overdone song...). As he often does, he made two recordings for the singer: one with the vocal line and another with just the accompaniment so he could properly learn the song. The following week, the tenor came in, proud that he knew the song backward and forward. When he finished singing it, David said, "Thank you, Aaron Tveit." Embarrassed, the singer said, "What do you mean?" David said, "I can tell you listened to the cast album. You're phrasing the song just like him."

You don't want another performer's version of the song you're singing to get stuck in your head (along with their phrasing, tempo, and even wrong notes and rhythms). For singers, it's very easy to mimic someone else. But, as great as Aaron Tveit is, the young tenor sounded a lot better when he wasn't doing his impression of him. Learn the piece on your own and then you can listen to others' performances for thoughts on interpretation.

For a quick outline of the above, see **Appendix H**.

### Other Ways to Prepare

There are many ways to prepare for a successful audition outside the practice room. All of the following things will elevate the work you're doing as a performer.

Pre Game

Preparing for audition day is no different from preparing for a sporting match. Have you ever seen an Olympic athlete before an event? They have their headphones on. They're turned away from the scoreboard. They're doing some sort of physical warm up. Every actor needs to create their own "pre-game" routine as well.

And it should include physical *and* mental preparation. Multiple Grand Slam tennis champion Serena Williams notes: "You win or lose the match before you even go out there."

Here are some recommendations as you prepare for your audition days:

- **Read up on the faculty**. (Re)read faculty members' bios so you can get a full picture of their experiences. It might spark some ideas for questions you'd like to ask at the audition.
- **Eat a good breakfast**. Auditions can take a *long* time. Hours. Just like an athlete, you need to keep your energy up so you're in peak form when it's your turn. Pack high energy snacks (protein bars, nuts, trail mix, jerky, etc...) and water (we're a fan of Smartwater or Vitaminwater Zero - both contain electrolytes, which are great for keeping you hydrated).
- **Plan what you will wear.** Don't overlook your outfit. An audition is like a job interview: your appearance will make a big impression. You should feel a bit dressed up. Dress appropriately for your age and sexual identity. Also consider your character type and the audition material you're going to perform. Wear shoes that are comfortable. (Ladies: If you plan to wear high heels to the audition make sure to rehearse in them.) Bright colors are great. If there's a dance call, those clothes should be separate from the rest of your audition attire. Check with each institution so you have a clear idea of the day's audition schedule. This will ensure you have time to change. And bring a back-up outfit, just in case.
- **Create playlists.** What music helps you relax? What music pumps you up? Create a few playlists you can listen to while you're sitting in the holding room to help you focus.
- **Prepare short warm-ups.** Beyond warming up for a dance call, it's also important to warm up your body to sing and speak. It can be a long time between home (or the hotel) and when you're slated to walk in for your audition. Create a warm up you can do in a hallway. Have the physical

warm up include something to get your energy up (jumping jacks, jogging in place) as well as things to get your mouth and voice active (we love tongue twisters!). Ask your voice teacher to record a 5-10 minute warm-up you can have on your phone. Some schools will give you a warm-up. That can be helpful too, but start with the warm-up you're accustomed to.

- **Visualize your audition**. Take some time to close your eyes and visualize your whole audition, from the time you walk in until the time you leave. What do you want to accomplish at this audition? See yourself getting to the end and feeling great about it after you leave. In the next chapter, we'll talk about how mindfulness can be a useful tool to see you through the long day of auditions.

## Your Music Binder

Make sure you have your entire audition book with you on each of your audition days. It's always a good idea to have other choices available to the adjudicators. Having said that, if it's in your audition book, it's fair game. So, if you currently have something in your book that's not ready for public consumption, take it out.

As mentioned in the previous chapter, you should always have two copies of each audition song: one full, unmarked copy, and another copy with clear markings of your 32- and 16-bar cuts (you should have both cuts marked, even if you plan to only do one of them).

How your audition cut looks on the page is very important. You'll only have about 30-40 seconds to speak to the pianist, so do the following to maximize your success:

- Clearly mark the beginning and ending of your cuts
- Avoid difficult page turns where possible
- Lightly highlight any important changes in the audition cut, such as tempo markings, time signatures, key signatures, etc...

See **Appendix I** for examples of good audition cuts.

Sheet protectors are not necessary, but if you're going to use them, it's time to invest in the right brand. Buy Avery Heavyweight Sheet Protectors, Non-Glare (Model# 74017). Non-glare sheet protectors are a must, as the regular sheet protectors make it almost impossible to see the music under bright lights.

## Talking to the Pianist

It's important you know how to clearly communicate information to your audition pianist.

Start by saying hello. Don't try to shake their hand or introduce yourself. It's not that they don't care, but the pianist's mind needs to focus on the pertinent information you'll be giving them. The longer you're at the piano, the more muddled the information becomes.

What should you tell them? The basics are simple: tell them the name of the piece you'll be singing, then think the acronym **BET**: Beginning, End, Tempo. You should tell them the name of the song you're singing, show them the beginning of the cut, the end of the cut, and give them the tempo. When giving the tempo, sing the beginning of your cut while gently tapping your thigh or other body part. Make sure to *never* snap your fingers at the pianist. If there's other specific information they need to know (i.e. - repeats, tempo changes), point these out last. Make sure important changes such as these are highlighted in the score to make life easier for the pianist. Then, ask if they have any questions before taking the stage.

If you're singing a pop/rock song, you should give the information in a slightly different order. Tell the pianist the name of the song and give the tempo from the hook (or chorus) of the song. This is very important because it's usually the hook of the song people remember. It also tends to be the less syncopated part of the song, making it easier to recall. When giving a tempo for a pop/rock song, you want to communicate both the speed at which you sing it and the style of the song. Don't be afraid to use your body a bit and show the groove. It will help the pianist, as most of the accompaniments to pop/rock songs are notoriously bad (Sheri Sanders is changing this. Again, visit her at rocktheperformance.com). After you've given the tempo, then show the pianist the beginning and end of the cut and highlight any other important information.

If you're singing more than one audition piece, show both cuts to the pianist at once unless otherwise instructed. This will save you from having to go back to the piano.

Remember: the pianist is there to help you! Most audition pianists are well versed in standard musical theatre repertoire. Keep in mind they've probably been playing all day. They may not seem like the friendliest creatures. Don't take any of that personally. Trust they know what they're doing and that you're in good hands.

***Also, be nice!*** Once, David was playing college auditions when a cocky baritone threw his binder open to "She Cries" from Jason Robert Brown's *Songs from a New World* (a definite no-no for auditions). He then proceeded to walk away without saying a word. David called him back and said (aloud for the adjudicators to hear), "This isn't one of those pieces you just set in front of a pianist and don't talk about." Visibly annoyed, the singer talked him through the audition cut. His performance was passable, but the adjudicators had already made up their minds: he wasn't coming to their school based on how he treated David. Don't blow your audition before you've sung a note - treat the pianist with the respect they deserve.

If something goes wrong (i.e. - an awkward start, incorrect tempo, etc...), always claim responsibility for it, apologize, and ask start again. Even if you're sure it's the pianist's fault, say it's your own. You want them on your side.

There's absolutely nothing wrong with starting over if you need to. This is your time to show who you are. Go back to the pianist and review the information you initially gave them, asking if they have any questions. Then start again.

Don't leave your audition book at the piano - that's a rookie mistake lots of young performers make because they're nervous. And be sure to thank the pianist for playing for you after you finish your audition, even if you didn't like the way they played.

## Your "Slate"

Your slate is how you introduce yourself to those adjudicating your audition. For songs, it should include your name, the song you're singing, and the show title (if applicable). For monologues, the character and show title are sufficient. You should practice your slate every time you run your songs and monologues because, aside from your greeting, it's the first thing those listening to you will hear.

Chances are you will be waiting a while to audition without speaking. Your slate is your last chance to get on your breath and voice before presenting your audition. Make sure to speak with a resonant voice. This will ensure you're already well placed to perform.

Most students inadvertently apologize for their existence, mumbling their slate. Not only does this not prepare them to perform, it doesn't engage the adjudicator(s). And don't you want them to pay attention?

Here's a sample slate:

Hi, my name is David Sisco [breathe], and I'll be singing "Giants in the Sky" from *Into the Woods*.

If you breathe after your name, it will ensure you don't rush and help you articulate the song and show title. Once you've properly slated, you will be ready to perform.

Some colleges will require a video pre-screen before assigning you a live audition date because of the high volume of applying students. The information above still applies to video auditions, but please see Chapter 8 for more information on videoing your submission.

## STUDENT

As Benjamin Franklin said, "By failing to prepare, you are preparing to fail."

In the first chapter of the book, we likened training in musical theatre to that of an athlete preparing for the Olympics. You must have incredible drive and endurance to be successful at your auditions. Practicing isn't necessarily fun or easy. It's process, not product. And yet, there's no way around practice if you truly want to be a consistent performer.

Think of performers whom you admire. We guarantee very few of them rose to success without practicing their craft. Even those who have had illustrious careers are still in the practice room, working with coaches, preparing for their next roles.

We want to point out that, beyond the technical challenges of learning your songs and monologues, you will also encounter mental and emotional stumbling blocks as you prepare your audition material. Singing and acting brings stuff up. You might have feelings of doubt or inadequacy. A character's given circumstances might remind you something you personally faced. All of this is completely normal, but don't let any of it stop you from the work of practicing.

How much should you be practicing? We think one hour five times a week is sufficient if you're starting when we suggested. If not, you may need to adjust your time table. Your teachers and coaches may have thoughts on this as well, so be sure to check with them.

You want to know every nook and cranny of your audition material. The only way to do that is to take it apart and get it in your body. Take the time to do this, and you will consistently perform well in your auditions.

When it comes to the audition day, you will most likely be stressed. It's normal. Make sure not to take that out on your parents. They're there to help. We often see students arguing with their parents at auditions and it doesn't bode well for anyone. If you're traveling with a teacher or friend instead, the same rules apply. Know when you need time apart and when you need their support. It's good to put a plan in place with your parent(s) beforehand, outlining what kind of support you need on audition day.

## TEACHER

Your job at this stage of the game is very important. Make sure the student shows you what each institution requests for audition material so you have a clear sense of how to help them prepare (See **Appendix A**).

Many students don't know how to properly learn a monologue or song. We offer **Appendix G and H** as samples of how to learn new material and encourage you to add your own ideas.

In addition, the student will most certainly need your help with all of the other logistical things that come with an audition: How do you talk to the people in the room? Where do I look? Can I ask questions? As a teacher or coach, it is your job not just to help your students learn the material, but teach them how to be present in the audition room. How to remain calm and listen to the questions or prompts they are given.

An audition is not just a chance for the auditors to hear how talented your student is. It's also a chance for them to find out a little more about who they are as people. You will help your students a lot by practicing the whole audition with them: from walking in the door until they leave the room, as outlined above.

Discuss what they plan on wearing. An audition is similar to a job interview. They should feel dressed up. Help make sure their attire is age and gender appropriate. If ladies want to wear high heeled shoes, make sure they rehearse in them.

After they sing, give them some feedback on the song and then give them an adjustment. For example, "That was great, but can you perform it again and pretend you're singing it to a very small child?" or "This time when you sing it can you make it sound like you're very confused" or "Can you turn this into a country song?" Let them know that getting an adjustment doesn't mean they've done something wrong. Adjudicators might just want to see how well they listen and take direction.

Also ask them what other songs they have in their book. Pick one and have them sing it. Let them know that they should not have anything in their book that is not ready to be sung at the audition.

Practice the interview section of the audition by asking some "wild card" questions (see **Appendix J**).

Tell your students there is no point trying to second guess what the adjudicators are looking for when they answer. Schools are looking to build a community as well as find talent they can nurture. They ask questions as a way of figuring out if your student will be a good fit for them. The best your student can do is relax, smile, look the adjudicators in the eyes, and confidently answer. You can help prepare them to be comfortable answering questions.

Laura routinely ends every coaching session with a few wild card questions. One student came back from her first college audition very confident because she had been asked some of the exact questions Laura had asked. Another student reported that he had been asked very different questions than any Laura had asked but, because he'd become used to routinely answering wild card questions in his weekly coaching sessions, he felt very comfortable answering and was happy with his responses. Remind your students that there are not "right" and "wrong" answers. The adjudicators are just looking for a chance to get to know them better.

In addition to the above, recording a 5-10 minute vocal warm-up they can do before each of their auditions will be supremely helpful. Some institutions will warm up the students before their singing audition, but they know *your* warm-up. Having you there with them - even on a voice memo - will be meaningful to them.

The more prepared they are for any situation, the calmer they will be at the audition. The calmer they are at the audition, the better they will perform. You will be an incredible resource for them during this eventful time.

## PARENT

While you may not be able to help your child prepare for auditions, you can certainly help them by keeping track of deadlines and audition requirements (**Appendix A**). Imagine yourself as the stage manager for your child's auditions. You're in charge of all logistics related to the audition dates: travel, hotel, food, clothes, snacks, etc... Essentially everything that is not artistic but allows your child to do their best.

The binder we recommended you create in Chapter 2 will be very useful to you here. You can include any paperwork about the audition itself (schools often send out confirmation letters with important information) along with travel and hotel confirmations. When questions come up or things go wrong (and they will), you'll have the answers right at your fingertips.

A word about traveling to auditions. Unfortunately, you'll be driving and flying during the winter months, which means unavoidable delays. It's important to avoid traveling the day of the audition, unless the institution is close by. Give yourself recovery time in the unfortunate event something goes wrong with your flight, or you have car trouble.

You might want to consider joining a hotel's honors program, since you'll potentially be booking a lot of hotel stays in the near future. It's quite possible to rack up enough points for a free night by the end of the audition tour. Also, if you're traveling to New York City, you might want to consider staying in New Jersey for cheaper hotel rates. Public transit is generally reliable and inexpensive. It might save you a fair amount of money in the long run.

If you get to the campus early enough the previous day, you might be able to take a tour of the school together. It's also not a bad idea to go to the audition space, just so you know exactly how to get there and your child has an opportunity to look around. Many times you won't have a chance to get a feel for the campus and program until the audition weekend.

You may also want to schedule an appointment with an admissions counselor to review your child's application and ask any outstanding questions. The more your child sees you taking an active role in this process, the better.

The evening before your child's audition, have an early dinner and a quiet night in. It's important they get plenty of rest and aren't too over-stimulated. We find it's best to schedule attending shows or other fun events *after* the audition, when the pressure is off. Everyone will enjoy the experience more.

Create a game plan for you and your family to set in motion each audition day. Make sure they eat a good breakfast the morning of the audition, and pack some snacks and water. Use the checklist in Chapter 7 to help them pack up. Planning ahead will keep everyone happy. Leave for the audition early, so no one feels rushed. The more your child can remain calm, the better their audition will be.

You know your child best. Do they crave quiet time to focus, or are they better if they are doing something energetic? Ask if they want you to drive them to the audition? And do they want you to wait with them?

Parents with a performing arts background are often frustrated when their own children don't want to take their professional advice. This is very tricky. While what you say may be very valid, it's hard for most young performers to separate the personal parent/child relationship with the professional coaching you might try to offer. Our advice? Hire an outside coach. It will cost some money, and they may not offer advice vastly different from yours. But it will help keep the peace.

Keep in mind that, when you attend your child's audition day, you're representing them. Plan to dress up the way you would for an interview. You'll be talking to faculty and students, so you'll want to look your best.

Remember how we said you'll be traveling in the winter months? As you know, that's cold and flu season. Keeping yourself and your child healthy is incredibly important. There's nothing worse than auditioning while sick. While it won't necessarily keep your child from being accepted to a program, performers tend to get in their heads when they're ill, which means they're less available to give the best performance.

Self care is a must for any professional artist. We're all being pulled in a thousand directions and can only be at our best when we're taking care of our body. That means getting lots of rest, eating well, drinking lots of (non-sugary) fluids, meditating... the list goes on. Help your child come up with a healthy lifestyle game plan they can incorporate prior to audition season. This will help keep them at their best.

Your job as a parent is to figure out how you can best support your child. Speak to them. Let them know you're available if they need you and maybe make suggestions of how you can support them through the process. Also keep in mind that they're, well, a teenager and emotions will be running high. They may get argumentative. Avoid making a scene at an audition. We see it happen quite a bit. Just know your child will probably be very stressed out and perhaps a little contrary. Try to go with the flow and and be a good "pit crew," anticipating their needs.

The audition tour should be the most enjoyable part of the journey. You have a rare opportunity to be with your child, away from the busyness of your lives, exploring different cities and colleges together. Make this time more special by planning ahead and making it something truly worth looking forward to.

# CHAPTER 7: AUDITION DAY CHECKLIST

We're excited for you! If you've taken the time to prepare as outlined in the last chapter, today doesn't need to be scary.

Here's what you need to remember for a successful audition day:

- ☐ **Eat a good breakfast/meal.** Avoid dairy, soda, or things that might upset a nervous stomach (citrus, coffee).
- ☐ **Make sure your audition book is in order.**
- ☐ **Bring your notes and questions about the school.** Bring a notebook, pens, and paper copy of audition day confirmations and instructions. Bring list of the faculty members' names.
- ☐ **Print out directions to audition and campus map.** You don't want to get lost and then find there's no wifi or cell reception.
- ☐ **Bring snacks, mints or gum, and water.**
- ☐ **Pack your audition outfit and dance clothes.** Also, bring all your dance shoes (you never know if they'll ask you to tap!), and a change of clothes in case of a clothing malfunction or spill.
- ☐ **Pack an "emergency kit"** (tape, toothbrush, hairbrush, bandages, safety pins, extra glasses or contact lenses, panty hose/tights, etc...).
- ☐ **Make sure your phone is fully charged and you have a battery backup and charger.**
- ☐ **Bring something to do.** There's lots of sitting around at auditions. Bring some Sudoko, crossword puzzles, coloring... whatever helps you relax.
- ☐ **Listen to your music playlist(s).**
- ☐ **Practice your slate for monologue and song(s).**
- ☐ **Practice talking to the pianist.**
- ☐ **Do a vocal warm up.**
- ☐ **Do a physical warm-up.**

# CHAPTER 8: WHAT HAPPENS ON AUDITION DAY?

We see it happen all the time. Students who have worked incredibly hard to give a great audition crumble under the pressure of a long and stressful audition day. So much focus has been put on their audition material that the information session, dance call, waiting in the hall before their audition, the interview, and all the other logistics of the day wipe the student out before they even sing a note or utter a word.

There's so much that goes into a successful audition beyond the audition time itself. This is one of those chapters you should read several times.

Pace Yourself

Audition days are long. They often include an information session, a dance audition, and a monologue and sung audition. It's not unreasonable to expect to be occupied the entire day. Keep your body and voice warm. Keep hydrated. Eat enough to keep your energy up.

A lot of information will be coming your way. This means you need to listen, take notes, mentally prepare for what's coming next, and let go of what you did well or maybe wanted to do better.

Be Yourself

As is true with any audition situation, you have no clue what the adjudicators are looking for. And the truth of the matter is that you're auditioning them as much as they are auditioning you. They know this is a difficult process and they want to see you succeed. While you're trying to put your best foot forward with a solid audition, they should be warm and hospitable, giving you a favorable impression of their program. If they're not, then that is a good indication that you might not want to go to school there. Take the opportunity to engage the auditors, if you can. Ask them questions (that you have, of course, prepared beforehand).

While you want to do well, your value is not fixed solely on one audition. When you're worried about what people think of you, you're physically and emotionally blocked from showing your true self. Have you ever had that out-of-body experience of watching yourself perform? You don't want to have that happen in your audition. Stay in the room (and in your body) by breathing and telling yourself: I AM ENOUGH..

And never underestimate how fun a day of auditions can be. You'll meet lots of new people your age who love doing what you do. There's a good chance you'll see some of these folks again - if not at this particular school, at an audition somewhere down the line.

On a cold February Saturday afternoon, David nervously stood outside an auditorium waiting to audition for graduate school. Ahead of him were a lovely couple: Sandra, a mezzo, and her husband Bill. Sandra was ready to transition from teaching music to a performing career and Bill, who was also a wonderful singer, was there to support her. After a friendly conversation, which calmed everyone's nerves, they went their separate ways.

Fast forward to the following Fall: both David and Sandra were accepted and decided to attend the same graduate school. They are now lifelong friends and support each other's successes.

You never know who you'll meet at your auditions and how your lives will continue to intertwine. Be yourself. The rest will follow.

Dealing with Anxiety

One of our favorite books is "There's a Monster at the End of this Book" with Sesame Street's lovable ole Grover. He thinks there's a monster at the end of the book and begs the reader not to turn another page. No matter how Grover tries to foil the reader from turning the pages, he is unsuccessful.

**Spoiler Alert**: It turns out Grover was the monster at the end of the book all along. The book ends with him saying, "And *you* were so afraid." Cute.

Fear can sometimes get the best of us in an audition situation. Yet, we are almost always our worst enemy - the monster at the end of the book. Many times, it's because we've stopped breathing. Most all our technical skill as singers is connected to the breath. Our objectives as actors are also connected to the breath. If you stop breathing, these things quickly diminish and the voices in your head will dominate. So, *breathe*. And repeat again: I AM ENOUGH.

Practice a short meditation. Close your eyes and picture yourself somewhere you find relaxing. Take a deep breath in through your nose, then exhale through your mouth while saying (or thinking) the word "Relax." Be mindful of any tension in your body and focus on that area on your next breath. Repeat for six breaths. At the end of this meditation, picture yourself walking into the audition and performing at your best. Then open your eyes. You're ready to go!

Can you start from a place of gratitude before you do your audition? Remind yourself that you love doing this and be excited to share what you do. Gratitude is always a wonderful antidote to fear.

## Sing for the Size of the Room

Loud is not impressive. Also, loud is not an emotion. Many young singers we've seen (at least half) give an American Idol-esque performance, trying to impress with piercing high notes. We often stop them after a couple measures. Everything you present in an audition is an acting opportunity. Dynamics are a direct reflection of the character's inner emotional life. If everything is loud, there's no emotional arc to the character's journey because everything is of equal importance. Varied dynamics will get the people behind the table to hear you better.

Sing for the size of the room. Some audition rooms are quite acoustically live. So when people loudly belt, we stop them to protect our ears (it's an important part of our careers after all!). Figure out the acoustic of the room when you slate and sing for that space. If the room is acoustically dead, it means you'll need to focus more on resonance to create your own ring, since the room isn't giving it to you. If it's live, it will be much easier to feel supported, which means you don't need to push.

## Your Monologue

By now, you should have several monologues that meet any time restrictions an institution might have. Set yourself up for success by ensuring you are under the time limit. Having said this, no one is going to remember the last word of your monologue. The point is not to get to the end (though that's optimal) - it's to play your action verbs and fight for what you want in the monologue. Take your time. Breathe. Honor the pace of the monologue as you've rehearsed it. This will allow the adjudicators to see you as a smart actor. Make sure you start and end strong. This does not mean loud, it means focused. Don't forget to take your moment before you begin to close your eyes and take a breath. Know who you are speaking to and where you are. And when you are done, make sure your last line feels final. Then gently drop your head, look straight at the people at the table, and say, "thank you."

## The Interview

Some institutions will interview you, either during or separate from your audition time, so they have a better sense of who you are as a young artist. They may ask you questions about yourself, your experience, or why you want to go to their school. Some schools may ask "wild card" questions like: "If you could be any animal, what would you be?" or "Of the musicals you have seen, which is your favorite? What did you love about it?" There are no right or wrong answers to these kinds of questions. Just try to relax, listen to the question, look at the person/people speaking to you and respond. They just want a chance to get to know you a little.

Look at **Appendix J** for common interview questions. Practice answering them (out loud!).

## When You're Done

It's common for students to rush out of the room after finishing their audition selection(s). We understand it's uncomfortable - you don't know what the adjudicators are going to say, if anything, but don't run away! They may want to ask you some questions. Sometimes they might want you to sing something else. All good reasons to stay put until you're excused.

Don't let what has or hasn't happened distract you. And don't discuss how the audition went as soon as you get out of the room. Casting directors often use their hall monitors as their eyes and ears during professional auditions. We have seen this work against actors. Colleges are likely to do the same thing. You don't want to finish a stellar audition and then be penalized for trash talking the pianist. Be professional and save the discussion and debriefing until you're in private and away from the venue.

Create a post-audition ritual that includes something positive. Call a supportive friend. Or give yourself a treat. One of our students liked to go for a favorite Starbucks drink after each audition. She allowed herself to think about the audition only as long as it took to finish the drink. Then she had to let it go.

And before you know it, this audition you've spent months (even years) working up to is done! "And *you* were so afraid..."

## Other Requirements

Some schools may require other individual audition tests such as music theory, keyboard or sight singing. While it is impossible to prepare for every eventuality, if you hear that one of your schools is requiring something unique, don't be shy about asking for details (i.e. What does this test entail? How long is it? What specific skills are you looking for?) You can usually find sample tests online to use as practice. Ask a teacher to help you prepare. As with all your audition material, remember that they are not looking for perfect artists - they are looking for artists with promise they can work with and train for the next four years.

Prepare as much as you can and then just be in the moment, listen to what is asked of you, and do your best.

## Pre-Screen & Video Auditions

There may be times when sending a video audition is your best bet. Some colleges require you to submit a pre-screen audition before assigning you an audition date because there are so few slots available for the. For others, time and finances may make traveling to the school an impossibility. Performing in person is always preferable, but many colleges take video auditions seriously.

We've seen a lot of poor video auditions. Read each school's video submission guidelines carefully. You may not be able to use the same video for all the schools, depending on the requirements. Here are a some other things to keep in mind when sending video auditions:

- It's completely acceptable to shoot a video on your smartphone. It's important, however, that you keep it stable - don't have mom or dad hold it while you perform! There are some inexpensive tripods on the market that will help make your video look more professional.
- Carefully consider where to shoot your video. It should be a neutral place that doesn't suggest a particular venue (home, school, church, etc...). Make sure the background of your video is not too busy. Otherwise, adjudicators will be look at what's on your mantlepiece instead of paying attention to you.
- Think about the room's acoustics and lighting. If the acoustic in the room is too live, it will be hard to understand you. You also don't want to appear in shadow or be washed out by too much light.
- Make sure three quarters of your body appears in the video. Your entire body is your instrument. And keep your movements limited so you don't go out of the frame.
- Remember to slate. Review the information above about giving a good slate. That applies here too.

- If performing a song, you must have a live accompanist. Performing acapella or with a track will look unprofessional.
- Shoot the video horizontally, not vertically. If you shoot it vertically, it will look strange when you upload it to YouTube or a similar website.
- Don't look straight at the camera. Pick a point slightly to the side.
- If possible, edit the video on iMovie or a similar application. Add your name, song and monologue titles. You can also include the school you're auditioning for (i.e., "Eliza Kaufman: Video Audition for Hamilton College.") Also, trim the video so it has a strong beginning and end.
- Do several takes so you have options of which to send.
- Be sure to watch your audition before sending it out! Review them with your teachers or coaches.

Unified Auditions

Unified Auditions are attended by multiple colleges and universities at a single venue in several major cities across the country. There are two different kinds of unified auditions: the first is a single audition in one hall for all of the schools attending and the second is a private appointment at the venue with the individual schools. In the latter case, appointments and interviews are made through the individual institution. There are several advantages of attending Unifieds: they allow you to audition for multiple colleges and universities in one location over several days (in Spring 2017 there were 28 schools attending). This is definitely a way to save time and money and get seen by a lot of schools in a short amount of time. Some schools will have "walk-in" spots available, so you can audition for schools you may not have known about.

There are several disadvantages to Unifieds as well. You probably won't get much information about the schools themselves since you're not visiting a campus or getting to talk to current students. It can be exhausting and intimidating to audition once for so many schools or do so many individual auditions in such a short period of time. We've heard from several students and parents alike that the audition day is relentless (a great piece advice from a parent: scope out the venue the day before the auditions and choose a home base). Given this, schools may not be able to give you as much time and attention as they would if you visited their campus. If you're easily nervous, this breakneck audition day might not be for you. And while the diversity and number of schools attending has grown in recent years, most likely all of the schools on your wish list won't be attending so you will still need to schedule individual auditions for those schools. But if time and cost are of concern, you may want to consider attending a Unified Audition. Search online for "unified auditions musical theatre" to find the location nearest to you.

## STUDENT

Most schools will have faculty and students on hand at auditions to guide you and answer questions. Take advantage of this. Try to spend time with the juniors and seniors who have more experience in the programs. Here are some questions you can ask:

- What opportunities have they had to perform both on and off campus?
- How many students are there in the program from their class year? How many students in the program overall?
- Do they have difficulty finding available practice rooms?
- What master classes has the department held?
- Is there a jury/cut process, in which students may be told they can not continue with the performance track?
- Have they been able to get into the classes they wanted/needed to?
- What opportunities are there to connect with agents, casting agents, and other industry professionals?

Remember, that you are auditioning the school as much as they are auditioning you. Take the opportunity to find out if this is a place you want to study and spend the next two to four years.

## TEACHERS

Discuss and practice the whole audition process including warming up and taming anxiety. Share your own personal experiences. Most likely you will not be with your students on audition day, so the best you can do is prepare them well and debrief with them after they return.

## PARENTS

The first thing you're going to want to ask your child after they auditioned is: "How did it go? Do you think you got in?" Avoid doing this, especially at the audition site. It might be better to say something like, "I look forward to hearing whatever you want to tell me about your audition when you're ready. I hope it went well."

The truth is, your child will still be processing what happened. As we said, audition days are incredibly long. They'll be tired and probably a little unsure of what to make of the whole thing (especially if it's their first audition). Giving them time to think about everything before talking about it will make for a better conversation.

Now is the time to do something fun. Take them out for a nice dinner, or to a show if you can. Young performers can often obsess over the smallest details of an audition day (i.e. - Why did the ask me to sing another song? Did I interview well?, etc...). The best thing is to take their mind off what just happened, regardless of how it went.

Here are some things you should not do:

- Don't be the parent trying to stand out on behalf of your child. If you have legitimate question to ask at an information session, of course ask it. But you don't want to be "that parent" who harasses the faculty. It might come back to haunt you child's chances of admission.

103

- Do not hover around the audition area. Your child needs space at this moment. It's hard to let go, but they need to do this alone. Hug and kiss them goodbye and let them focus on the work ahead.
- Do not gossip with other parents about this (or other) schools. Sometimes the other students' parents can be more dramatic than their children, wanting to share audition horror stories or compare notes on other schools your child is considering. *Do not engage.* Keep the conversation light and breezy, or move on. You don't know who has connections where. Say as little as possible and try to cordially exit the conversation.

Some things you should do:

- Stay positive and help your child relax and stay in the present moment. Auditions are stressful. If you see them getting anxious, help them get back on track. Have a game plan with your child about how they would like you to support them on audition day.
- Instead, take copious notes at the information session, write down the names of the people you meet, look for selling points and possible red flags. When in doubt, write it down. You're going to receive a lot of information, and it will begin to blur with other programs. It's great to have notes to look back on. After the audition, compare notes with your child. You'll be interested to see they experience through their eyes.
- Set a time after each audition to discuss it and debrief (we will discuss this more in Chapter 9). Encourage them to make notes to keep them with their audition materials. They can revisit them in preparation for their next audition.

Other things you can do:

- Talk to current students at the university
- Explore the campus
- Ask Admissions and Financial Aid Office any unanswered questions

- Schedule something enjoyable for yourself, making sure to be close by when your young artist is done with their audition.

A dad of a (now) college musical theater freshman suggested that being a good listener (not an analyst) is your top priority. It might be tempting to show enthusiasm for one school over another because of *your* experiences and inadvertently pressure your child as a result. Avoid setting your child up for potential disappointment. Instead, rank the schools in order of preference based on all the information you're collectively gathering. This list should be started before you even start auditioning. Then once they start auditioning, encourage them to enjoy the journey and trust the process. Gather information and revisit your rankings. Once the acceptances start coming in, you can revisit your list and factor in things like financial aid and scholarships.

# CHAPTER 9: WHAT NEXT?

And now you wait. In some ways, waiting to hear back from the institutions where you auditioned is the most challenging part of this whole process. At least when you're preparing, you have clear goals and a long "to do" list. After all that's done, it will feel like you're at the institution's mercy.

You hopefully know roughly when you'll hear from each institution. If you don't, it's OK to call and ask. But you shouldn't ask for feedback on the audition itself. And frankly, others' advice at this point will only get you in your head. Every audition you do will be unique. If you have good teachers in place, trust their guidance and your own intuition about how the audition went.

Some students will write an email thanking the adjudicators for their time. This is not necessary and will often not get a response (think of all the prospective students doing the same thing). Trust that your "thank you" in the audition room was enough.

Here are some proactive things to focus on while you're waiting to hear back from each institution.

Journal

Hopefully, you jotted down some notes during the audition day. If you didn't, do this as soon as you can - you want to remember every moment, as it will help you down the road. We'll talk about evaluating the audition a little later. For now, focus on the the institution itself:

- What did you learn about the institution you didn't know before?
- Was the administration, faculty, and student community welcoming?
- What did you like most about your experience there?
- Did you see any potential drawbacks?
- Would you rank the institution differently based on your experience?

When in doubt, write it down. In some cases, you won't come back to these notes for several weeks or even a couple months. The simplest thing might help jog your memory of whether or not the school was a good fit.

Compare Notes

Everyone should compare notes after journaling. Students, teachers, and parents will all notice different things. Pool your notes so you can develop a more well-rounded picture of the institution.

When discussing advantages and drawbacks, you'll need to collectively weigh the information. Maybe living in the dorms furthest from the arts campus isn't a big drawback if you'll have access to state-of-the-art practice rooms. Consider why you chose this institution in the first place, and see if it's still meeting your initial expectations. Many times, what you see in the glossy school brochures is not what you experience on audition day. It's important to note these differences.

Research Financial Aid

Hopefully, you've already spent a lot of time getting to know each of the institutions where you applied and auditioned. Now is the perfect time to better understand how you'll be paying for your education.

Understanding financial aid for college can feel daunting because there are so many moving parts: loans, scholarships, grants... It's confusing. And yet, you need to educate yourself so you can make smart decisions about your educational debt, which has the potential to be with you for quite a while (we're still paying off our student loans and we're... not exactly young!).

Have a family member or guidance counselor help you begin to understand how financial aid works. You can also visit studentaid.ed.gov and financialaidtoolkit.ed.gov. These sites will walk you through everything from why a college education is important to what types of financial aid you might qualify for.

You'll also want to visit FAFSA.gov (Free Application for Federal Student Aid), which gives out out Pell Grants, a subsidy from the US Federal Government to help pay for college. Students can qualify for Pell Grants for up to 12 semesters of study.

FAFSA forms must be submitted by **June 30** prior to your first semester. Some institutions will require you to fill out this form, regardless of your financial picture, because it influences their own aid at the state level. We were told many times there is money left over each year, so you'll want to be sure and utilize this great (free) resource. Remember: you don't have to pay grants back. That's a big deal, and a big savings.

You should research the institutions where you applied, finding out how much money they give out in academic and "talent" scholarships. **Important**: make sure you understand how your scholarship will be applied. Some institutions will only promise scholarships for the Freshman year, just to get students in the door. Others will offer academic and "talent" scholarships for all four years. Make sure you understand what each institution offers.

During this time, you should also be looking for scholarships to augment what the institution may give you. You can start doing this as early as the summer before your senior year. Your guidance counselor should be a great resource, but be sure to search on your own as well. Check out other online resources like collegescholarships.org and fastweb.com. Most of the information you'll find here is also completely free.

The more of your education you can pay upfront, the better. Apply to any scholarship or award you can, even if it's only for a couple hundred dollars. That will be enough to cover books your first semester (yes, they're that expensive!).

You may have to submit a video of yourself performing in tandem with certain scholarship applications. If you didn't have to create a video audition for a pre-screen or general submission, review Chapter 8 for insights on how to do this.

Most institutions will have work-study programs, which will support you while you're in college. Work-study programs allow students to take on part-time jobs at the institution (i.e. working in the admissions office, the library, etc…) while taking classes. This gives the student a little more financial freedom. Work-study usually is determined as part of the financial aid package and a dollar amount is set for each semester. It's up to the student to apply for the job and work the hours to earn the money. Ask each institution for more information about how they handle work-study.

Understanding the financial picture of your education is just as important as the education itself. Be proactive now and it will serve you very well in the future.

**Making the Decision**

Once the letters start coming in, you'll need to formulate a game plan. Many students work so hard on applying, writing essays, preparing for and giving the auditions that they completely forget their work is far from done once the auditions are over. They may become understandably paralyzed with the fear of making the wrong choice. This is where all the research you've done in the last several months will be of ultimate use to you. Review the spreadsheet you created along with your notes about each college.

Unfortunately, we can't help you with this part. We can, however, offer some friendly advice. Certainly, scholarship and financial aid packages will help inform your decision, but they shouldn't be the only considerations. Here are some other things to think about:

- What institution do you feel will offer you the most growth?
- Where did everyone feel most "at home"?

- What school offered the best overall package, including: curriculum, faculty, facilities, and performance opportunities?

Hopefully, the answer to these questions will help narrow the decision down.

Sometimes you'll want to see if you can get more financial support before making a final decision. Understand that many schools have their own rubric for figuring out how much scholarship and financial aid to give a student, which is based on many factors (such as household income, etc…). Financial aid officers get bombarded with requests because everyone wants a more money. Add into that the fact that many people don't know how to have this conversation, which only exacerbates the problem.

The student should write a letter (not an e-mail) to the financial aid office requesting additional financial support. They must convincingly outline why this particular school is the right choice for their education and why, and what they could bring to the university community. Refrain from using words like bargaining or negotiating. That's not what you're doing. You're asking the financial aid office to reconsider the initial offer.

The student should then follow up with a phone call. From our research, it seems financial aid officers were more apt to work with students who were being proactive than parents who acted on their child's behalf.

Be tenacious, but not obnoxious. Schools have discretionary funds set aside for these eventualities, but that doesn't necessarily mean you'll get more money. Be ready for the institution not to budge. But knowing why and how to ask will increase your chances.

There are two fantastic New York Times articles you should Google: "Appealing to College for More Financial Aid" (April 4, 2014) and "How Colleges Know What You Can Afford (and the Limits of That Tactic)" (May 17, 2017). Both have incredibly helpful advice to guide you through these rough waters.

In Chapter 1, we talked about students migrating from program to program in search of what they were wanting in their education. Take time to carefully consider which program will best speak to your needs while balancing the other important aspects. It will save you time and a lot of money in the future.

Oh, and congratulations! Take a moment to celebrate all you've accomplished together. Being accepted into one or more musical theatre programs is a *huge* deal. You should feel a sense of pride in your achievements!

## STUDENT

While you're waiting to hear back from the places you auditioned, use your time wisely. In addition to journaling about the school, you should ask yourself the following questions specific to your audition:

- What did you wear? (Was it appropriate? How did it compare to others auditioning? Were you comfortable? Would you wear it again for another audition?)
- What did you sing? (How was it received? How did the pianist play? How well did you communicate the beginning, ending, and tempo? Did the adjudicator(s) offer any feedback? What would you do differently?)
- What monologue(s) did you perform? (How was it received? How was the pacing of your performance? Did you honor the beats you had practiced? Did you find your moment before? Did the adjudicator(s) offer any feedback? What would you do differently?)

Once you've journaled about the audition itself, review some logistical things about the day:

- How did you manage your energy throughout the day?
- Was there anything that threw you for a loop?
- Did you arrive to the audition site early enough? Too early?
- Were there any questions you forgot or were afraid to ask?

And finally, check in with your gut about the entire experience:

- How were your nerves?
- Did the entire day go as you thought it would? What was less or more challenging?
- Do you feel you did your absolute best? If not, what could you do differently to mentally and emotionally prepare for your next audition?

Did you know that some professional musical theatre performers do much of the same thing when auditioning for casting directors? They want to remember what "the room" was like: was it friendly or cold? They also want to remember what they wore and performed so they can either choose to repeat those options (in the hopes of jogging the casting director's memory) or do something different. Getting into the habit of journaling about your auditions can serve you well throughout your career.

Some of this information will simply be for you and your teachers or coaches. You may consider sharing other parts with your parents if it's relevant to how you would rank the institution. That's your decision to make.

## TEACHER

You have an opportunity to keep the student focused on the process of their development as a young artist. Like many young students, they may be more concerned they haven't yet heard back from their school of choice. Help guide their energy toward something more useful: the continued development of a healthy technique. Regardless of the outcome, this information will not be wasted.

Ask the student what they learned about themselves through their audition. Maybe the song they chose didn't illuminate who they are. Maybe they received feedback from the adjudicators they should lead with something else. This should help guide you on what to work on next as they prepare for future auditions.

A student may want to check out at this point, thinking they know all their audition material. We like to remind our clients how important it is to keep all the audition material "fresh." They will have to perform this material under many different circumstances in varied spaces. The more they continue to practice, the better equipped they will be for most eventualities. It will at least make them more present when things don't go according to plan.

Inevitably, the student will ask your opinion about attending one school over another. Remind them that the decision has to be their own. While you might have personal preferences based on experience, it may stand in the way of the student discovering the school that's best for them.

David had a superior experience during his undergraduate degree, but that was... a while ago. Is that particular program still strong? Maybe, or maybe not. Likewise, David had a very negative experience during graduate school. Should he keep his students from attending for the same reasons?

Our students value our thoughts more than we sometimes know. We must be careful to be supportive without projecting our personal biases.

## PARENT

In addition to hoping your child will be accepted to the college of their choice, you will feel the added pressure of wondering what their financial aid package will look like.

One of the things we wished we had better understood was the expense associated with getting a college degree. Financial aid is a confusing but unavoidable component of higher education. You and your child can learn more about this together. It will give them an appreciation of the financial sacrifices it may take for them to go to college and inspire them to be proactive about looking for scholarships and grants.

It will be tempting to let the scholarship and financial packages dictate where your child goes to school. We recognize the cost of a college education is monumental and that fears on how to manage the expense are well founded. It can't, however, be the driving force behind a decision that will affect your child's life for years to come.

When it comes to deciding where to go, allow your child to explain their thoughts. This is an opportunity for you to stand back and watch them become an adult. If they've done their homework, they'll have strong opinions on where they should go to school. You may have strong opinions too, and your opinions matter. Hopefully, you will be able to come to an agreement.

We hope this process has allowed you to more clearly see your child's passion, talent, and fortitude. And we're sure that, in you, they will see a parent that loves and supports them. Congratulations to you all!

We've done our best to give you as much information as possible in a concise way. And yet, as we said at the outset, we only experience certain things sitting behind the table.

So, we reached out to current and former students in musical theatre programs around the country to ask them what they wished they had known going into auditions. They reminded us of some other little tidbits that will be helpful as you prepare.

## *Practice, Practice, Practice*

Work with a teacher weekly and practice every day. You want know all your material inside out. Perform your audition material in front of friends and family. The more you comfortable you are in front of people, the better you will do at your audition. It is also a good idea to work with an accompanist who is not your voice teacher so you can practice talking through your audition cuts.

## *Wear Comfortable Clothes & Shoes*

Of course, you want to look nice, but you also need to be comfortable. Audition days are long. Wear something presentable that you'll also be fine wearing for the entire day. And a change of clothes is never a bad thing, just in case.

Make sure you can properly inhale in your outfit and you feel comfortable moving in it - don't wear anything too tight. Don't wear a new pair of dance shoes for your audition just because they're pretty - you could end up hurting your performance. Make sure you can do a combination in them without sacrificing technique. Women, if you wear heels, they should similarly be broken in. Make sure you practice your audition in them, as they will affect everything from your posture to intentions.

That doesn't mean what you wear has to be boring or predictable. In fact, it should be quite the opposite. Show your personality and put your best foot forward with a well-planned audition outfit. It will tell the adjudicators you're serious about presenting yourself in the best light.

## *You are What You Eat (and Drink)*

Consider eating protein the day of your audition (i.e. eggs, turkey sausage, etc...). Avoid dairy and carb-heavy meals that might make you feel bloated or tired later on. Pack some protein bars or other snacks that won't leave crumbs or stick in your teeth (pack a toothbrush to be safe). You might even want to do a dry run of some possible audition day meals and snacks to discover what works best for you.

Where beverages are concerned, water is a good choice. Smartwater and Vitaminwater Zero (both by Glacéau) are great because they contain electrolytes, which keep you hydrated. This will help you maintain over the course of a long audition day.

Tea can be good as well, but no coffee, soda, and other carbonated drinks on audition day, as they could potentially dry you out.

## *When It's Done -- It's Done!*

Don't spend tons of time after the audition over analyzing your performance and beating yourself up. Be happy you got the chance to show them who you are.

## *Create a Separate Email for School Correspondences*

You might be a little embarrassed to have admissions people email you at bunnylover02@gmail.com. Create a separate email address expressly for college correspondences. It will make you look more professional and ensure you don't miss any important information.

## Don't Rank Your School Choices

While this is something we recommended in a previous chapter, one student recommended not ranking the schools because it can create hurt feelings later on if you don't get accepted.

This really depends on the kind of person you are. You may find, though, that a school who wasn't even on your radar has become a very strong option the more you get to know them. Don't create absolutes (i.e. - I *must* go to Carnegie Mellon...), and you'll be fine.

## Communicate with Your Teachers About Possible Absences

You and your family will be traveling a lot over the course of the audition season. It's quite likely you'll miss more than a couple days of school. Make sure to keep your teachers and school administrators aware of why you're absent and keep on top of missed work.

\*\*\*\*

Thank you for letting us be part of your lives as you prepare for this exciting and challenging time. We hope you found this book helpful and are confident in incorporating what we've talked about to give successful auditions.

One final reminder: no one is you. There is not a single person on this earth that is an amalgam of your particular gifts, experiences, and personality. And who you are will forever change. The same is true for your teachers, parents, and even those sitting behind the table.

With so much in flux, what can we do but truthfully be who we are in the moment and share our passion with great love?

Every song you sing, every word you utter, "Let it come from you," as Dot reminds the artist at the end of *Sunday in the Park with George*. "Then it will be true." And what could be more beautiful than that?

119

# APPENDIX

# APPENDIX A
*College Audition Spreadsheet*

Below is a sample spreadsheet young artists and parents should create together to keep track of the many deadlines and requirements each school has. We've included some fun inside jokes for musical theatre geeks like ourselves on these completely fabricated institutions. Enjoy finding them!

Of course, you should feel free to modify this to your own needs. You might find other categories that are important to your particular situation. By all means, add them.

|  | Sondheim School of the Arts | Andrew Lippa University | Jerry Herman Conservatory |
|---|---|---|---|
| Type of College | Conservatory | Liberal Arts | Conservatory |
| Type of Degree | BFA | BA | BFA |
| Notes | Has a stronger dance component. | 60 credits in the major and 60 credits in the college, balanced. | This curriculum seems more geared toward contemporary musical theatre and pop/rock styles. |
| Website | www.ssa.edu/musicaltheatre | alu.edu/dramadepartment | jhconservatory.edu/arts/mtheatre |
| Admiss. Contact/ Tel. | Johanna: (992) 234-5678 | Kate: (323) 134-8972 | Cornelius: (212) 699-3444 |
| App. Fee | $30 | $50 | $30 |
| Admiss. Deadline | 2/6/17 | 1/15/17 | 1/1/17 |
| Admiss. Notes | 11/5 - Spoke to Johanna in the admissions office - confirmed application was complete and all is | 11/6 - Missing one rec. letter - f/u with Mrs. Schroyer next week. | 10/31 - School confirmed receipt of transcripts. Waiting on SAT scores. Audition yet to be scheduled. |

|  | Sondheim School of the Arts | Andrew Lippa University | Jerry Herman Conservatory |
|---|---|---|---|
|  | set for her 2/6 audition. |  |  |
| **Audition Date** | 2/6/17 | 2/22/17 | TBD |
| **Audition Loc.** | On Campus | Las Vegas - Unifieds | On Campus |
| **Audition Reqs.** | • 1 MT song written before 1970 (16-32 bars) <br> • 1 classical piece written before 1900 (full song) | • 1 Golden Age legit MTsong (16 bars) <br> • 1 contemporary (c. 2000) MT song (16 bars) | "If you sing in a legit and belt voice, you may sing two selections. Otherwise, prepare one 16-bar cut that shows off your voice." |
| **Audition Day Notes** | • Friendly faculty <br> • Loved the campus <br> • Pianist had a hard time with my up-tempo | • Amazing dorms <br> • They don't have practice rooms!! <br> • The adjudicators asked me to sing my 32-bar ballad | • Arrived late, wasn't ready for my audition <br> • We auditioned as a group, not one-by-one <br> • The head of the program made me nervous |
| **Accept. Date** | Two weeks after my audition. | March 30 | February 15 |
| **Fin. Aid** | Received a $10K academic award, but only for the first year | Waiting to hear about talent scholarship | Received $3,500 award for each year. |

Below are a list of summer musical theatre intensives offered in the United States and a few abroad. This is not a comprehensive or recommended list. Ask your teachers if they know of other opportunities in your area and make sure to research the intensives as you would a college program.

| Program | State | Mailing Address |
|---------|-------|-----------------|
| The Broadway Experience | CA | Harvey Milk Center for the Arts City of San Francisco Recreation and Parks 50 Scott Street San Francisco, CA 94117 |
| California State Summer School for the Arts | CA | California State Summer School for the Arts PO Box 1077 Sacramento, CA 95812-1077 |
| UCLA Summer sessions | CA | 1331 Murphy Hall Los Angeles, CA 90095-1418 |
| USC Musical Theatre Intensive | CA | 649 W. 34th St., Suite 108 Los Angeles, CA 90089-1627 |
| Perry-Mansfield Pre-Professional Intensive | CO | 40755 County Road 36 Steamboat Springs, CO 80487 |
| Theatre Aspen Summer Conservatory | CO | Theatre Aspen: Main Office 110 East Hallam Street. Suite 103 Aspen, CO 81611 |
| Broadway Theatre Project | FL | University of South Florida College of the Arts 4202 East Fowler Avenue Tampa, FL 33620-7450 |
| Sam Houston State University: The Broadway Artist's Intensive | FL | Sam Houston State University Huntsville, Texas 77341 |

| Program | State | Mailing Address |
|---------|-------|-----------------|
| Atlanta - Buford Musical Theatre Intensive | GA | 2705 Robert Bell Parkway Buford, GA 30518 |
| Kennesaw State University Summer Arts Intensives | GA | 1000 Chastain Road Kennesaw, GA 30144 |
| National High School Institute, Cherubs (Northwestern University) | IL | 617 Noyes Street Evanston, IL 60208 |
| Midsummer Theatre Program, Indiana University | IN | Indiana University Dept. of Theatre and Drama 275 North Jordan, Room A300U Bloomington, IN 47405 |
| AMDA High School Summer Conservatory | LA | AMDA - LA CAMPUS 6305 Yucca Street Los Angeles, CA 90028 |
| ArtsBridge Summer (MT concentration) | MA | 185 Crescent Street, Suite 301 Waltham, MA 02453 |
| Boston Conservatory at Berklee | MA | 8 Fenway Boston, MA 02215 |
| Boston University Summer Theater Institute | MA | Boston University Summer Theatre Institute Boston University College of Fine Arts 855 Commonwealth Avenue, Room 470 Boston, MA 02215 |
| Emerson Pre-College Musical Theater Program | MA | 120 Boylston Street Boston, MA 02116-4624 |
| Walnut Hill School Summer Theater | MA | 825 Walnut Street Philadelphia, PA 19107 |

| Program | State | Mailing Address |
|---------|-------|-----------------|
| Interlochen Summer Arts Programs | MI | Interlochen Center for the Arts<br>Office of Admission and<br>Financial Aid<br>P.O. Box 199 (US Mail)<br>9900 Diamond Park Rd.<br>(FedEx, UPS, DHL)<br>Interlochen, MI 49643 |
| Mpulse Summer Performing Arts Institutes (University of Michigan) | MI | 2230 Moore Building<br>1100 Baits Drive<br>Ann Arbor MI 48109-2085 |
| North Carolina School of the Arts: Drama Summer Session | NC | 1533 S. Main Street<br>Winston-Salem, NC 27127 |
| Triple Arts at Western Carolina University | NC | Nantahala National Forest<br>1 University Way<br>Cullowhee, NC 28723 |
| Rutgers Summer Acting Conservatory | NJ | Mason Gross Extension Division<br>Rehearsal Hall 101<br>85 George Street<br>New Brunswick, NJ 08901 |
| Westminster Choir College High School Musical Theatre Intensive | NJ | 101 Walnut Lane<br>Princeton, NJ 08540 |
| AMDA High School Summer Conservatory | NY | AMDA - NY CAMPUS<br>211 West 61st Street<br>New York, NY 10023 |
| Atlantic Acting School Summer Intensive | NY | Atlantic Acting School<br>76 Ninth Avenue, Suite 537<br>New York, NY 10011 |
| Broadway Artist Alliance | NY | 262 West 38th Street, Suite 504<br>New York, NY 10018 |
| The Broadway Experience | NY | 150 Joralemon Street, #4F<br>Brooklyn, NY 11201, USA |
| Fordham University Summer Musical Theatre Intensive | NY | Lincoln Center<br>33 West 60th Street<br>New York, NY 10023 |

127

| Program | State | Mailing Address |
|---|---|---|
| Joffrey Ballet School Summer Intensive | NY | Joffrey Ballet School 434 Avenue of the Americas 5th floor New York, NY 10011 |
| Ithaca College Summer College for HIgh School Students (introduction to musical theatre performance) | NY | Summer College for High School Students Ithaca College Office of International and Extended Studies 953 Danby Road Ithaca, NY 14850 |
| New School Summer Onstage Music Theatre Acting Intensive | NY | 66 West 12th Street New York, NY 10011 |
| New York Film Academy Musical Theatre Intensive | NY | 17 Battery Place, New York, NY 10004 (mailing address) 26 Broadway, 12th Floor New York, NY 10004 (Battery Park Location) |
| Pace University | NY | Office for Student Success One Pace Plaza, 2nd Floor Room Y21 New York, NY 10038 |
| Purchase College: Pre-College Musical Theatre Boot Camp | NY | Purchase College Music Building, Ground Floor 735 Anderson Hill Road Purchase, NY 10577 |
| StageDoor Manor | NY | 15 StageDoor Drive Loch Sheldrake, NY 12759 |
| Steinhardt NYU Summer Study in Music Theatre | NY | MPAP Summer Programs 35 West 4th Street, Suite 1077 New York, NY 10012 |
| Stella Adler Musical Theatre Intensive | NY | 31 West 27th Street, Floor 3 New York, NY 10001 |

| Program | State | Mailing Address |
|---|---|---|
| Syracuse University Summer College for High School Students | NY | Syracuse University Summer College for High School Students 700 University Avenue Syracuse, NY 13244-2530 |
| TISCH SUMMER HIGH SCHOOL DRAMA PROGRAMS (New Studio Summer Music Theatre Program) | NY | Office of Special Programs Tisch School of the Arts 721 Broadway, 12th Floor New York, NY 10003 |
| Wagner Summer Music Theatre Institute | NY | Wagner College Summer Music Theatre Institute One Campus Road Staten Island, New York 10301 |
| Musical Theatre Overtures - Baldwin-Wallace | OH | Community Music School Music Theatre Overtures Baldwin Wallace University 275 Eastland Road Berea, OH 44017 |
| University of Cincinnati CCM Preparatory Department High School Musical Theatre Intensive | OH | 3860 Corbett P.O. Box 210236 Cincinnati, OH 45221-0236 |
| Carnegie Mellon University Pre-College Program (Drama) | PA | Office of Admission Warner Hall 5000 Forbes Avenue Pittsburgh, PA 15213 |
| Penn State Musical Theatre Intensive | PA | Penn State School of Theatre 116 Theatre Building University Park, PA 16802 |
| Summer Institute - The University of the Arts | PA | 320 South Broad Street Philadelphia, PA 19102 |
| SFA School of Theatre Summer Theatre Workshop | TX | School of Theatre Stephen F. Austin State University P.O. Box 6090, SFA Station Nacogdoches, TX 75962-6090 |

| Program | State | Mailing Address |
| --- | --- | --- |
| Texas Arts Project - Musical Theatre | TX | 6500 St. Stephens Drive Austin, TX 78746 |
| Texas Musical Theatre Workshop | TX | Texas Musical Theatre Workshop c/o Lyn Koenning Artistic Director Winship Drama Building 300 E 23rd Street, Stop D3900 Austin, TX 78712 |
| Overtures - Signature Theatre | VA | Signature Theatre The Village at Shirlington 4200 Campbell Avenue Arlington, VA 22206 |
| Virginia Commonwealth University Pre-College Summer Intensive | VA | Virginia Commonwealth University 325 North Harrison Street Richmond, VA 23284-2519 |
| Arts Club Musical Theatre Intensive | Canada | 1. Surrey Arts Centre 13750 88 Avenue Surrey BC V3W 3L1 2. Goldcorp Stage at BMO Theatre Centre (Vancouver) - 162 West 1st Avenue Vancouver BC V5Y 1A4 |
| MusikTheatre Bavaria | Germany | Musiktheater Bavaria P.O. Box 545 Winter Park, FL 32790-0545 |
| The Broadway Experience | Italy | Attn: Gea Stramacci Lydia Turks Dance & Musical Via Marcello Provenzale 24 Rome, Italy |

## APPENDIX C
*Overdone or Inappropriate Songs*

It's impossible to list every song that may be either overdone or inappropriate. The list of writers, shows, and songs that go in and out of fashion changes all the time. When in doubt, consult a musical theatre professional about what (not) to perform.

### Anthologies to Avoid
1. Hal Leonard Singer's Musical Theatre
2. Hal Leonard Singer's Musical Theatre "16-Bar" Audition

### Composers to (Generally) Avoid
1. Jason Robert Brown
2. Michael John LaChiusa
3. Stephen Sondheim
4. Frank Wildhorn

### Shows to Avoid
1. *Any show currently running on Broadway*
2. *The Addams Family* (Lippa)
3. *Annie* (Strouse & Charnin)
4. *Cats* (Webber)
5. *Dogfight* (Pasek & Paul)
6. *Edges* (Pasek & Paul)
7. *The Fantasticks* (Schmidt & Jones)
8. *Grease* (Jacobs, et. al.)
9. *The Last Five Years* (Brown)
10. *Les Misérables* (Boubil & Schönberg)
11. *The Light in the Piazza* (Guettel)
12. *Newsies* (Menken & Feldman)
13. *Phantom of the Opera* (Webber)
14. *Rent* (Larson)
15. *Spring Awakening* (Sheik & Sater)
16. *Thoroughly Modern Millie* (Tesori/Scanlan)
17. *Wicked* (Schwartz)
18. *Wild Party* (Lippa)

131

## Overdone Songs

*Soprano or High Belt/Mix Songs*
1.  Astonishing (*Little Women*)
2.  Breathe (*In the Heights*)
3.  Gimme, Gimme (*Thoroughly Modern Millie*)
4.  The Girl in 14G (Jeanine Tesori & Dick Scanlon)
5.  Gorgeous (*The Apple Tree*)
6.  Green Finch and Linnet Bird (*Sweeney Todd*)
7.  Here I Am (*Dirty Rotten Scoundrels*)
8.  How Could I Ever Know? (*The Secret Garden*)
9.  If I Loved You (*Carousel*)
10. Moonfall (*Mystery of Edwin Drood*)
11. Mr. Snow (*Carousel*)
12. Much More (*The Fantasticks*)
13. My New Philosphy (*You're a Good Man Charlie Brown*)
14. My White Knight (*The Music Man*)
15. Part of Your World (*The Little Mermaid*)
16. Pretty Funny (*Dogfight*)
17. Show Off (*The Drowsy Chaperone*)
18. Taylor the Latté Boy (Marcy Heisler & Zina Goldrich)
19. Watch What Happens (*Newsies*)
20. Vanilla Ice Cream (*She Loves Me*)

*Mezzo Songs*
1.  Adelaide's Lament (*Guys & Dolls*)
2.  Don't Rain on My Parade (*Funny Girl*)
3.  Dyin' Ain't So Bad (*Bonnie & Clyde*)
4.  Journey to the Past (*Anastasia*)
5.  Lost in the Brass (*Band Geeks*)
6.  Maybe This Time (*Cabaret*)
7.  Memory (*Cats*)
8.  Pulled (*The Addams Family*)
9.  Screw Loose (*Cry Baby*)
10. Shy (*Once Upon a Mattress*)
11. Spark of Creation (*Children of Eden*)
12. Stranger to the Rain (*Children of Eden*)
13. Times Like This (*Lucky Stiff*)
14. Way Back to Then (*Title of Show*)

*Tenor Songs*
1. All I Need is the Girl (*Gypsy*)
2. Being Alive (*Company*)
3. Go the Distance (*Hercules*)
4. Grow for Me (*Little Shop of Horrors*)
5. Her Voice (*The Little Mermaid*)
6. I'm Alive (*Next to Normal*)
7. I'm Not That Smart (*... Spelling Bee*)
8. The Lady Must be Mad (*Illyria*)
9. Larger than Life (*My Favorite Year*)
10. Mama Says (*Footloose*)
11. My Unfortunate Erection (*...Spelling Bee*)
12. Purpose (*Avenue Q*)
13. Run Away with Me (*The Unauthorized Biography...*)
14. Santa Fe (*Newsies*)
15. Take a Chance on Me (*Little Women*)
16. This is the Moment (*Jekyll and Hyde*)
17. Tonight at Eight (*She Loves Me*)

*Baritone Songs*
1. Johanna (*Sweeney Todd*)
2. I Think I Like Her (*Summer of '42*)
3. If I Loved You (*Carousel*)
4. Oh, What a Beautiful Morning (*Oklahoma!*)
5. Once in Love with Amy (*Where's Charley?*)
6. Purpose (*Avenue Q*)
7. Some Enchanted Evening (*South Pacific*)

## APPENDIX D
*Song Recommendations by Voice Type*

Similar to Appendix C, these songs will also go in and out of fashion. We hope this short list will get your imagination going about other songs that might be appropriate for college auditions.

*Legit Soprano*
1. Alive (*A Proper Place*)*
   Contemporary Dramatic Uptempo

2. Falling in Love with Love (*Boys from Syracuse*)
   Golden Age Dramatic Ballad

3. He's Only Wonderful (*Flahooley*)
   Golden Age Dramatic Ballad

4. I Remember (*Evening Primrose*)
   Golden Age Dramatic Ballad

5. I Wish it So (*Juno*)
   Golden Age Dramatic Ballad

6. I Never Said I Love You (*Dear World*)
   Golden Age Dramatic Ballad

7. It Wonders Me (*Plain and Fancy*)
   Golden Age Dramatic Midtempo

8. My Sky (Adam Overett)*
   Contemporary Midtempo

9. Once You Lose Your Heart (*Me and My Girl*)
   Golden Age Dramatic Ballad

10. Take Me to the World (*Evening Primrose*)
    Golden Age Dramatic Ballad

11. When Did I Fall in Love (*Fiorello*)
    Golden Age Dramatic Midtempo

12. Will You Know Me? (*Rochester Knockings*)*
    Contemporary Dramatic Ballad

*High Belt/Mix*

1. Be a Little Wild (*Like You Like It*)*
   Contemporary Pop/Rock Uptempo

2. Feelings (*The Apple Tree*)
   Golden Age Comic Midtempo

3. Hold My Hand (Jeff Blumenkrantz)
   Contemporary Dramatic Ballad

4. Horizon Line (*Stone and Sparrow*)*
   Contemporary Dramatic Ballad

5. I Love a Cop (*Fiorello!*)
   Golden Age Comedic Ballad

6. I'm Not (*Little by Little*)*
   Contemporary Comic Uptempo

7. If You Hadn't But You Did (*Two on the Aisle*)
   Golden Age Comic Uptempo

8. Isn't It? (*Saturday Night*)
   Golden Age Comic Uptempo

9. Never Gonna Be a Waitress (*Kira*)*
   Contemporary Dramatic Uptempo

10. One Foot on the Ground (*Placebo*)*
    Contemporary Dramatic Ballad

11. Poor Little Hollywood Star (*Little Me*)
    Golden Age Dramatic Ballad

12. Saturday Alone (*Calvin Berger*)*
    Contemporary Dramatic Ballad

*Legit Mezzo*

1. Bewitched (*Pal Joey*)
   Golden Age Dramatic Ballad

2. The Boy Next Door (*Meet Me in St. Louis*)
   Golden Age Dramatic Midtempo

3. But Not for Me (*Girl Crazy*)
   Golden Age Dramatic Ballad

4. It Might as Well Be Spring (*State Fair*)
   Golden Age Dramatic Ballad

5. In Our Time (Leonard Bernstein)
   Golden Age Dramatic Ballad

6. Lay Down Your Head (*Violet*)
   Contemporary Dramatic Ballad

7. Look Who's in Love (*Redhead*)
   Golden Age Dramatic Ballad

8. Love of My Life (*Brigadoon*)
   Golden Age Comic Uptempo

9. Make Him Mine (*Neurosis: The Musical*)*
   Contemporary Comic Ballad

10. My Own Space (*The Act*)
    Golden Age Dramatic Ballad

11. Simple (*Nine*)
    Golden Age Dramatic Ballad

12. You Will Be Inside My Heart (*Sara Crewe*)*
    Contemporary Dramatic Ballad

## Belt Mezzo

1. Another Life (*Dance a Little Closer*)
   Golden Age Dramatic Ballad

2. Beyond Words (*Stone and Sparrow*)*
   Contemporary Dramatic Midtempo

3. Door/Window (*The Yellow Wood*)*
   Contemporary Dramatic Ballad

4. Hittin' the Road (*Minnesota*)*
   Contemporary Pop/Rock Uptempo

5. I Enjoy Being a Girl (*Flower Drum Song*)
   Golden Age Comic Midtempo

6. I Think That He Likes Me (Kooman & Dimond)
   Contemporary Comic Uptempo

7. Let's Play a Love Scene (*Fame*)
   Contemporary Dramatic Ballad

8. Nobody Does it Like Me (*Seesaw*)
   Golden Age Comic Ballad

9. Right in Front of Your Eyes (*The Wedding Singer*)
   Contemporary Pop/Rock Midtempo

10. Slightly Perfect (*Are You With It?*)
    Golden Age Comic Uptempo

11. Someone Woke Up (*Do I Hear a Waltz?*)
    Golden Age Dramatic Uptempo

12. There's a World Out There (*Little Women*)*
    Contemporary Dramatic Uptempo

*Legit Tenor*
1. Be with Me (*Like You Like It*)*
   Contemporary Dramatic Ballad

2. Beautiful City (*Godspell*)
   Golden Age Dramatic Ballad

3. I Cannot Hear the City (*Sweet Smell of Success*)
   Contemporary Dramatic Ballad

4. I Don't Want To (*All Shook Up*)
   Jukebox Dramatic Ballad

5. If You Ever Think of Me (*D. Copperfield*)*
   Contemporary Dramatic Ballad

6. Sing to Me (*My Life is a Musical*)*
   Contemporary Dramatic Ballad

7. That's for Me (*State Fair*)
   Golden Age Dramatic Midtempo

8. A Thousand Miles (*Pride and Sensibility*)*
   Contemporary Dramatic Midtempo

9. What Can you Lose? (*Dick Tracy*)
   Golden Age Dramatic Ballad

10. What More Do I Need? (*Saturday Night*)
    Golden Age Comic Uptempo

11. With Anne on My Arm (*La Cage Aux Folles*)
    Golden Age Dramatic Midtempo

12. You Remind Me of Home (*The Tavern Keepers...*)*
    Contemporary Dramatic Ballad

*Belt Tenor*
1.  All I Want (*The Longing and the Short of It*)*
    Contemporary Comic Uptempo

2.  Disappear (*The Burnt Part Boys*)
    Contemporary Dramatic Uptempo

3.  Extraordinary (*Pippin*)
    Golden Age Dramatic Uptempo

4.  Florida (Brad Alexander & Helen Chayefsky)*
    Contemporary Dramatic Uptempo

5.  Fly at Me (*Little Women*)*
    Contemporary Dramatic Uptempo

6.  It Just Wasn't Meant to Happen (*Calvin Berger*)
    Contemporary Dramatic Uptempo

7.  Lost in the Wilderness (*Children of Eden*)
    Contemporary Dramatic Uptempo

8.  No One Goes to an Amusement... (*Action Park*)*
    Contemporary Comic Ballad

9.  Rock City (*See Rock City and Other Destinations*)*
    Contemporary Pop Musical Theatre

10. What I Wouldn't Do for You (*Mrs. Sharp*)
    Contemporary Dramatic Midtempo

11. Why (*Tick, Tick... BOOM!*)
    Contemporary Dramatic Midtempo

12. You're Different (*Violet*)
    Contemporary Dramatic Ballad

*Baritone*
1. Disappear (*Burnt Part Boys*)
   Contemporary Dramatic Uptempo
2. I Can See It (*The Fantasticks*)
   Golden Age Dramatic Uptempo
3. Love Walks In (*Ceremony*)*
   Contemporary Dramatic Ballad
4. Lucky to Be Me (*On the Town*)
   Golden Age Dramatic Ballad
5. The Man I Used to Be (*State Fair*)
   Golden Age Comic Midtempo
6. Moments of You (David Sisco & Tom Gualtieri)*
   Contemporary Dramatic Midtempo
7. Nothing Can Stop Me Now (*The Roar of the...*)
   Golden Age Dramatic Uptempo
8. Mr. Potato Head (*Calvin Berger*)*
   Contemporary Comic Ballad
9. What More Do I Need? (*Saturday Night*)
   Golden Age Dramatic Uptempo
10. Why Can't I Kiss You? (Jeff Blumenkrantz)
    Contemporary Dramatic Ballad
11. This Eve (*The Apple Tree*)
    Golden Age Comic Midtempo
12. Your Eyes are Blue (cut from *Forum*)
    Golden Age Dramatic Ballad

**\* - Available for purchase on ContemporaryMusicalTheatre.com**

## Writers to (Generally) Avoid

1. Christopher Durang
2. Jules Feiffer
3. Beth Henley
4. Neil Labute
5. David Mamet
6. John Patrick Shanley
7. Theresa Rebeck
8. Nicky Silver
9. Neil Simon
10. Wendy Wasserstein

## Books to Avoid

*The Actor's Book of Contemporary Stage Monologues*
by Nina Shengold

## Shows to Avoid

1. *A... My Name is Alice*
2. *Boy's Life*
3. *Brighton Beach Memoirs*
4. *Danny and The Deep Blue Sea*
5. *Equus*
6. *Five Women Wearing the Same Dress*
7. *The Fantasticks*
8. *For Colored Girls....*
9. *In the Boom Boom Room*
10. *How I Learned to Drive*
11. *Our Town*
12. *Proof*
13. *A Raisin in the Sun*
14. *Rabbit Hole*
15. *Steel Magnolias*
16. *Suburbia*
17. *Talk Radio*
18. *Talking With*

19. *This is Our Youth*

20. *You're A Good Man Charlie Brown*

## Overdone Monologues

*Women*

1. *Agnes of God* by John Pielmeier (Agnes): "Where do babies come from?"

2. *Assassins* (Squeaky Fromme): "I was like you once. Lost. Confused... "

3. *The Fifth of July* by Lanford Wilson (Shirley): "I'm going to be the greatest artist Missouri has ever produced..."

4. *Getting Out* by Marsha Norman (Arlie): frogs monologue

5. *A Girl's Guide to Chaos* by Cynthia Heimel (Cynthia): "Dating. I will have to start dating again."

6. *Gruesome Playground Injuries* by Rajiv Joseph (Kayleen): "You can't marry that girl, Doug. You can't."

7. *Happy Birthday, Wanda June* by Kurt Vonnegut (Wanda June): "Hello I'm Wanda June and today was going to be my birthday..."

8. *An Ideal Husband* by Oscar Wilde (Mabel): "Well, Tommy has proposed to me again. Tommy really does nothing but propose to me..."

9. *Slow Dance on the Killing Ground* by William Hanley (Rosie): "If you knew me better, you'd see that this is exactly the kind of thing that's likely to happen to me."

10. *Stop Kiss* by Diana Son (Callie): "They're finished building that building across from your apartment. Wake up now. Sara. Can you hear me? Open your eyes."

*Men*

1. *Ah Wilderness* by Eugene O'Neill (Richard): "Must be nearly nine.... I can hear the Town Hall clock strike..."

2. *Angels Fall* by Lanford Wilson (Zappy): tennis monologue

3. *Buried Child* by Sam Shepard (Vince): "I was gonna run last night."

4. *A Chorus Line* (Paul): "From seeing all those movie musicals, I used to dance around on the street..."

5. *The Glass Menagerie* by Tennessee Williams (Tom): "What do you think I'm at? Aren't I supposed to have any patience to reach the the end of, Mother?"

6. *I Hate Hamlet* by Paul Rudnick (Andrew): "To be or not to be..."

7. *Red* by Yasmina Resa (Ken): "Bores you?! Bores you?! Christ almighty, try working for you for a living!"

8. *Red Light Winter* by Adam Rapp (Matt): "How to start... Let's see..."

9. *Rosencrantz & Guildenstern are Dead* by Tom Stoppard (Rosencrantz): "Do you ever think of yourself as actually dead, lying in a box with the lid on it?"

10. *Take Me Out* by Richard Greenberg (Mason): "I've been watching baseball nonstop since the day I was told you were coming to me..."

144

*Monologue Recommendations by Genre*


*Comedic Men*
1. *After Math* by Jonathan Dorf (Shaking Student): "Mrs. Parks has this thing about tests."

2. *Class Action* by Brad Slaight (Dennis): "My name is Dennis Gandleman."

3. *Everything Will Be Different* by Mark Schultz (Freddie): "Um. Hi. Charlotte. Um. Okay I know this is awkward and everything."

4. *The Innocents Brigade* by Keith Reddin (Bill): "You see I have all this talent."

5. *Last Day of School* by Ian McWethy (Brian): "I'm just...I guess I'm just having a hard time Dave."

6. *Square One* by Mark D. Kaufmann (Darren): "A couple days ago I knew exactly what I'd say up here."

7. *Stress, Pressure, Doom and Other Teen Delights* by Alan Haehnel (Jack): "Can I help it that I am surrounded by collegiate geniuses?"

8. *Techies* by Don Goodrum (Charlie): "Anthony, you have to help me! What am I going to do?"

9. *A Tiny Miracle with A Fiberoptic Unicorn* by Don Zolidis (Louis): "She's never gonna like me."

10. *When it Rains Gasoline* by Jason D. Martin (Jessie) "You guys just don't get it. We just need to remember our roots."


*Dramatic Men*
1. *...And the Rain Came To Mayfield* by Jason Mulligan (Carl): "You know this is funny..."

2. *Blink of An Eye* by Debbie Lamedman (Jeremy): "When I get outta here--first thing I'm gonna do is go visit Mom."

3. *The Dark at the Top of the Stairs* by William Inge (Sammy): "It's awfully nice of you to let me take you to the party"

4. *A Life of Pieces* by David Minyen (Matthew): "Why do we do this? Why is it that we always wait for something like this to happen to us before we take action?"

5. *The Matchmakers* by Don Zolidis (Gabe): "You know why I like astronomy?"

6. *Praying for Rain* by Robert Louis Vaughan (Marc): "Like... What was my history?"

7. *Second Class* by Bradley Slaight (Leon): "If you listen closely... you can hear the past."

8. *Skid Marks: A Play About Driving* by Lindsay Price (Greg): "I promise I won't snot on my arm this afternoon. I have a hankie on me."

9. *Spring* by Tanya Palmer (Mitch): "You didn't expect to see me again, I know."

10. *Valentine's Day* by Horton Foote (Horace): "When I was nine I had some chickens that I raised as pets."


*Comedic Women*

1. *All The Girls Hate Me at West Haddock High* by A.M. Dittman (Allison): "You know, I think maybe I will go to the dance with you."

2. *A Bird of Prey* by Jim Grimsley (Hilda): "I don't hate him or anything..."

3. *Charming Princes* by Emily C.A. Snyder (Cinderella): "Fairy Godmother, listen to me..."

4. *Circumvention* by Anton Dudley (Anna): "Don't laugh at me..."

5. *The Diary of Adam and Eve* by Marc Bucci (Eve): "Sunlight? Hummingbirds? Lions? Where am I? I? What am I? OH!! Whatever I am, I'm certainly a beautiful one."

6. *The 1st Annual Achadamee Awards* by Alan Haehnel (Connie): "Mom, please sit down."

7. *Last Day of School* by Ian McWethy (Katie): "Yes of course I do. You just... you just accused me of being a super cool mean girl."

8. *Last Night in London* by Kimberly Lew (Jill): "My roommates and I went to Rome."

9. *Second Class* by Bradley Slaight (Mirelle): "Thank God this is the last year I'm going to have to go through this."

10. *The Staggering Heartbreak of Jasmine Merriwether* by Don Zolidis (Jasmine): "No. I'm rushing things."

## Dramatic Women

1. *Billboard* by Michael Vukadinovich (Katelyn): "On the plane I sat next to this little girl and her mother."

2. *Blink* by Phil Porter (Sophie): "When I look at myself I can see myself like normal."

3. *The Cradle Song* by Gregorio Martinez Sierra (Theresa): "Do you know how I would like to spend my life? All of it?"

4. *Finer Noble Gases* by Adam Rapp (Dot): "In the library at my junior high they have these huge computer monitors."

5. *The Less Than Human Club* by Timothy Mason (Kirsten): "You're a wonderful dancer..."

6. *Pretty Theft* by Adam Szymkowicz (Allegra): "I know you're probably mad at me..."

7. *Sally's Gone, She Left Her Name* by Russell Davis (Sally): "I miss mom coming into my room at night."

8. *The Secret Garden* by Isabella Russell-Ides (Mary Lennox): "Your eyes are beautiful. It's odd—when I try to remember Mother's face, it's like looking in a foggy mirror."

9. *Six* by Timothy Mason (Selena): "Science used to be so much fun..."

10. *When We Were Young and Unafraid* by Sarah Treem (Penny): "Why? What am I doing wrong?"

*Six Steps to Learning a New Monologue*
Laura Josepher

1. **Read the play**
   a. A monologue is out of context. There is so much character and situational information you will not get from a monologue book such as who your character is talking to and what happened in the moments before. Read the play and take notes.
2. **Break it down**
   a. Choose one action verb that could be applied to the whole monologue.
   b. Break down the monologue into individual beats. Each time the action changes it is called a "beat." Go through the monologue and mark each new thought with a slash ("/")
   c. Attach an "action verb" to each individual beat
3. **Create your "moment before"**
   a. What happened right before your monologue?
      i. Where are you?
      ii. Who is with you in the scene?
      iii. What did another character say to your character to launch you into your monologue?
4. **Learn the monologue - don't memorize**
   a. Read the monologue out loud, then put the paper face down and say as much of the monologue as you remember. Next, pick up the paper again and read the monologue out loud again and identify what you remembered and what you forgot. Go back and forth between reading and performing. Using this method you will learn material faster and better understand what you're saying.
   b. Be sure you eventually learn the words exactly. Don't paraphrase at your audition!
5. **Write out the monologue out by hand**
   a. Studies show writing by hand strengthens the learning process.

        b.   You will quickly see where you are paraphrasing.

**6. Strong beginning and end**

        a.   Take time (5-10 seconds) before you start your monologue.

              i.   Close your eyes. Take a deep breath. Imagine your "moment before."

             ii.   Open your eyes. Focus on a spot eye level (not right at any one person) and "see" the character you are speaking to. Begin your monologue.

        b.   At the end of your monologue, make sure your last line feels final. Then gently drop your head, look straight at the people at the table, and say, "thank you."

*Six Steps to Learning a New Song*
David Sisco

1. **Research the song.**
    a. Art song: read the poet and composer's biography and find out when and why the piece was written.
    b. Opera or musical: read the scene in which the aria or song takes place. Consider reading the entire libretto and any source material.
2. **Write out the text by hand.**
    a. Make sure to write it out as a monologue, not as lyrics or poetry. Notice how it appears on the page, separate from the music.
3. **Recite the text as a monologue (see Appendix G)**
    a. Read the text aloud at different speeds, paying attention to where you breathe.
    b. Endow the text with "Shakespearean intent" - reciting the text with sense of heightened language will prepare you for singing.
    c. Focus on breath connection and honest language.
4. **Learn the rhythm by intoning and the melody by singing on a lip trill, ni or n + vowel.**
    a. Intoning is extended, energized speech without a musical pitch.
    b. After intoning the entire song, mix and match the other exercises throughout, discovering which ones help you in different sections of the song.
    c. Take your time with this step. Taking apart the song this way will allow you to bring your full technique to the piece.
5. **Translate the text into your own words.**
    a. Sung text is often poetic. You must find the essence behind each phrase and clearly communicate it.
    b. Translate the text line by line then try a real-time translation while singing (it doesn't have to rhyme or have the same amount of syllables).
6. **Mark the high point of each phrase in the score.**

151

a. Remember high notes are not always the high point of the phrase.
b. Notice if this changes where you breathe or how you experience the meaning of the phrase.

# APPENDIX I
*Sample Audition Cuts*

Included here are three different examples of audition cuts: 16-bar (consecutive), 16-bar (copied and paste) and 32-bar. Note how easy they are for the pianist to read.

## 16-bar cut (consecutive)

"You Don't Know Love" from *Falling to Earth*
Music by: David Sisco
Lyrics by: Tom Gualtieri
*Reprinted with permission*

This is the simplest scenario for an audition cut: singing the last section. You'll notice this 16-bar cut is actually 20 measures long. Not a problem. Remember: always finish the thought in your audition cut.

Make sure to lightly cross off any music that is not pertinent to your audition cut. Also bracket off the start of the audition cut and write "BEGIN," just to avoid any confusion. The cut is only two pages, which will allow you to place it in your binder without making the accompanist turn a page. These kinds of details are very much appreciated.

As noted above, highlight any important changes in the music, such as metronome mark, meter and time signature. This will draw the accompanist's eye to them when sight reading, helping them to support you better.

Again, your accompanist will be playing hundreds of songs the day of your audition - do anything you can to make their lives easier.

## 16-bar cut (spliced)

### Moments of You

Lyrics by: Tom Gualtieri

Music by: David Sisco

did-n't miss your hand or the sound of your voice read-ing

Stein-beck at "The Strand." I was wait-ing out the rain

in a ca - fé on Bleeck - er, and I did-n't feel the pain.

That was the morn - ing I for - got you said good bye. I'll take

**A** Highlight key change

"Moments of You"
Music by: David Sisco
Lyrics by: Tom Gualtieri
*Reprinted with permission*

In this cut, you'll notice we skipped from page 2 to page 5. It just so happened that removing the first chorus and second verse of the song made for a very clean audition cut. This is unusual. Splicing a cut like this will most likely require more pages. Wherever possible, consolidate by cutting extraneous music out and pasting the audition cut together. If you have access to Finale, Sibelius, or someone who uses these programs, they may be able to create cleaner audition cuts for you. This isn't absolutely necessary, but can be very helpful. Use your judgment and put all your auditions cuts in front of a professional (preferably a knowledgeable voice teacher or vocal coach) before your audition.

Also notice that this cut is 23 measures long, featuring a full verse, pre-chorus, and chorus. Again, this is OK. As mentioned in Chapter 6, many contemporary songs don't cut as easily as their Golden Age counterparts. As long as you deliver your song with conviction, the folks behind the table won't be counting measures.

When stopping in the middle of the song, make sure to mark "END" and cross out any music that isn't pertinent to your audition cut.

### 32-bar cut

less and less... I'm get - ting by... but still,................... I can't....

for - get........ Walk-ing Se-cond A - ve - nue,........

...............that song by Ni-na Si mone,........ or-chids in.... the win -

dow, the smell of..... Cop-per-tone, wak - ing up... a lone..........

"
Moments of You"
Music by: David Sisco
Lyrics by: Tom Gualtieri
*Reprinted with permission*

This is an exact 32-bar cut featuring the bridge, chorus and coda of the song. Make sure to mark the score as notated in each of these three examples.

161

Some institutions will interview you, either during or separate from your audition time. Try to relax, listen to the question, and look at the person who spoke to you.

1. Tell us something about yourself that has nothing to do with theatre.
2. Why do you want to come to our school?
3. What other schools have you applied to? *
4. Of the musicals you have seen which is your favorite? What did you love about it?
5. What shows have you performed in? What was your favorite role and why?
6. What are you looking to get out of this program?
7. Who is your acting idol?
8. What are your strengths and weaknesses?
9. Do you have any special skills you can show me?
10. Why do you want to be an actor?
11. Why did you choose your monologue/song?
12. What questions do you have for us?**

* This is an unfair question to ask, but we know colleges ask it anyway. You can avoid a direct answer by talking about what you're looking for in a school, and that their institution exemplifies those qualities.

**Always have a question prepared that can't be answered by looking at their website. It will show you to be a smart performer.

163

## APPENDIX K
*School Score Card*

You may want to develop your own system of grading each institution, but if you need a template, feel free to fill this out.

| | |
|---|---|
| *School Name* | |
| *Website* | |
| *Degree* | |
| *Number of Students* | |
| *Performance Opportunities* | |
| *Location/Commute/Campus* | |
| *Facilities (dorm + studios)* | |
| *Classroom Visit* | |
| *Talk to a Student* | |
| *Watched a Show* | |
| *Diversity* | |
| *Program Reputation* | |
| *Student Support* | |
| *Things I Loved* | |
| *Things I Didn't Like* | |
| *Other Observations* | |

45544141R00101

Made in the USA
Middletown, DE
07 July 2017